Dumb Show

Joe Penhall

Methuen Drama

Published by Methuen Drama

1 3 5 7 9 10 8 6 4 2

First published in 2004 by
Methuen Publishing Limited

Copyright © Joe Penhall

The author has asserted his moral rights

A CIP catalogue record for this book is available from the British Library

ISBN 0 413 77480 5

Typeset by SX Composing DTP, Rayleigh, Essex

ROYAL COURT

Royal Court Theatre presents

DUMB SHOW

by Joe Penhall

First performance at the Royal Court Jerwood Theatre Downstairs
Sloane Square, London on 2 September 2004.

DUMB SHOW

by **Joe Penhall**

Cast in order of appearance
Barry **Douglas Hodge**
Liz **Anna Maxwell Martin**
Greg **Rupert Graves**

Director **Terry Johnson**
Designer **Es Devlin**
Lighting Designer **Bruno Poet**
Sound Designer **Ian Dickinson**
Assistant Director **Claire Lovett**
Assistant Designers **Penny Challen, Howard Lloyd**
Casting Director **Lisa Makin**
Production Manager **Paul Handley**
Stage Manager **Sarah Waling**
Deputy Stage Manager **Nicole Keighley**
Assistant Stage Manager **Rebecca Austin**
Costume Supervisor **Iona Kenrick**
Company Voice Work **Patsy Rodenburg**
Set built by **Rupert Blakeley**
Set painted by **Charlotte Gainey**

THE COMPANY

Joe Penhall (writer)
For the Royal Court: Pale Horse, Some Voices.
Other theatre includes: Blue/Orange
(RNT/Duchess/Broadway); The Bullet (Donmar);
Love and Understanding (Bush, Off-Broadway);
Some Voices (Young Vic, Off-Broadway).
Television includes: The Long Firm, Go Back Out.
Film includes: Enduring Love, Some Voices.
Awards include: Olivier Award Best Play, Evening
Standard Award Best Play, Critics' Circle Award Best
Play (Blue/Orange), Thames Television Award (Pale
Horse), John Whiting Award (Some Voices).

Es Devlin (designer)
For the Royal Court: Credible Witness, Yard Gal.
Other theatre includes: Dog in the Manger, Antony
and Cleopatra, Henry IV, The Prisoner's Dilemma
(RSC); Hinterland, Betrayal (RNT); Five Gold Rings
(Almeida); Flag:Burning with Jake and Dinos
Chapman; Wire (Barbican); A Day in the Death of
Joe Egg (Comedy/Broadway); Arabian Night (ATC);
Rita, Sue and Bob, Too/A State Affair (Out of
Joint/Soho); Piano (TPT Tokyo); Airsick, Love and
Understanding, Howie the Rookie (Bush); The Death
of Cool (Hampstead); Hamlet (Young Vic); Perapalas
(Gate); Meat (Theatre Royal, Plymouth); Closer to
Heaven - the Pet Shop Boys musical (Arts); Edward
II (Bolton Octagon).
Film includes: Brilliant!, Snow on Saturday and
Victoria Station.
Opera includes: Macbeth (Klangbogen Festival,
Vienna), Powder her Face (Ystad Festival, Sweden),
Fidelio (English Touring Opera), Hansel and Gretel
(Scottish Opera Go Round).
Dance includes: Four Scenes, God's Plenty
(Rambert); A Streetcar Named Desire (Northern
Ballet Theatre); I Remember Red (Cullberg Ballet,
Sweden).
Awards include: nominated for TMA Best Design
2000 (Meat), Winner of TMA Best Design 1999
(Howie the Rookie), Winner of the Linbury Prize
for Stage Designer 1996 (Edward II).
Es is currently working on Hecuba for the RSC, and
operas including Orphee for the Royal Opera
House Linbury Theatre, A Midsummer Night's
Dream for Hamburg State Opera, L'Incoronazione
di Poppea for Houston Grand Opera, Nabucco for
Basel Stadium, and Don Giovanni for Klangbogen
Vienna.
Her work can be viewed at www.esdevlin.com.

Ian Dickinson (sound designer)
For the Royal Court: Shining City, Lucky Dog, Bless
Be the Tie, The Sweetest Swing In Baseball, Ladybird,
Notes on Falling Leaves, Loyal Women, The Sugar
Syndrome, Blood, Playing the Victim, Fallout, Flesh
Wound, Hitchcock Blonde (& Lyric), Black Milk,
Crazyblackmuthafuckin'self, Caryl Churchill Shorts,
Imprint, Mother Teresa is Dead, Push Up, Workers
Writes, Fucking Games, Herons, Cutting Through
the Carnival.
Other theatre includes: Port (Royal Exchange,
Manchester); Night of the Soul (RSC Barbican); Eye
of the Kappa (Gate); Crime & Punishment in
Dalston (Arcola Theatre); Search & Destroy (New
End, Hampstead); Phaedra, Three Sisters, The
Shaughraun, Writer's Cramp (Royal Lyceum,
Edinburgh); The Whore's Dream (RSC Fringe,
Edinburgh); As You Like It, An Experienced Woman
Gives Advice, Present Laughter, The Philadelphia
Story, Wolks World, Poor Superman, Martin
Yesterday, Fast Food, Coyote Ugly, Prizenight (Royal
Exchange, Manchester).
Ian is Head of Sound at the Royal Court.

Rupert Graves
Theatre includes: A Woman of No Importance
(Theatre Royal Haymarket); The Elephant Man
(Broadway); The Caretaker (Comedy); Closer
(Broadway); The Iceman Cometh (Almeida);
Hurlyburly (Old Vic/Queens Theatre); Les Enfants
Paradis (RSC); Design for Living (Gielgud); A
Midsummer Night's Dream, 'Tis Pity She's a Whore
(RNT); The Pitchfork Disney, A Madhouse in Goa
(Bush/Lyric, Hammersmith/Apollo); The History of
Tom Jones (Palace Theatre, Watford); The
Importance of Being Earnest (Crucible, Sheffield);
Candida, The Killing of Mr Toad (King's Head);
Amadeus (Theatr Clwyd); Torch Song Trilogy
(Albery); Sufficient Carbohydrate
(Hampstead/Albery).
Television includes: Charles II, Forsyte Saga, Take a
Girl Like You, Cleopatra, Blonde Bombshell, The
Tenant of Wildfell Hall, Open Fire, Royal
Celebration, Inspector Morse, Una Question Privat
Fortunes of War, A Life of Puccini, Good and Bad at
Games, St Ursula's in Danger, Union Matters,
Starting Out, The Children.
Film includes: Extreme Ops, Dreaming of Joseph
Lees, Mrs Dalloway, Revenger's Comedies, Intimate
Relations, Different for Girls, Innocent Sleep, The
Madness of King George, Damage, Where Angels
Fear to Tread, The Sheltering Desert, A Handful of
Dust, Maurice, A Room with a View.

THE ENGLISH STAGE COMPANY AT THE ROYAL COURT

The English Stage Company at the Royal Court opened in 1956 as a subsidised theatre producing new British plays, international plays and some classical revivals.

The first artistic director George Devine aimed to create a writers' theatre, 'a place where the dramatist is acknowledged as the fundamental creative force in the theatre and where the play is more important than the actors, the director, the designer'. The urgent need was to find a contemporary style in which the play, the acting, direction and design are all combined. He believed that 'the battle will be a long one to continue to create the right conditions for writers to work in'.

Devine aimed to discover 'hard-hitting, uncompromising writers whose plays are stimulating, provocative and exciting'. The Royal Court production of John Osborne's Look Back in Anger in May 1956 is now seen as the decisive starting point of modern British drama and the policy created a new generation of British playwrights. The first wave included John Osborne, Arnold Wesker, John Arden, Ann Jellicoe, N F Simpson and Edward Bond. Early seasons included new international plays by Bertolt Brecht, Eugène Ionesco, Samuel Beckett, Jean-Paul Sartre and Marguerite Duras.

The theatre started with the 400-seat proscenium arch Theatre Downstairs, and in 1969 opened a second theatre, the 60-seat studio Theatre Upstairs. Some productions transfer to the West End, such as Terry Johnson's Hitchcock Blonde, Caryl Churchill's Far Away, Conor McPherson's The Weir, Kevin Elyot's Mouth to Mouth and My Night With Reg. The Royal Court also co-produces plays which have transferred to the West End or toured internationally, such as Sebastian Barry's The Steward of Christendom and Mark Ravenhill's Shopping and Fucking (with Out of Joint), Martin McDonagh's The Beauty Queen Of Leenane (with Druid Theatre Company), Ayub Khan Din's East is East (with Tamasha Theatre Company, and now a feature film).

Since 1994 the Royal Court's artistic policy has again been vigorously directed to finding and producing a new generation of playwrights. The writers include Joe Penhall, Rebecca Prichard, Michael Wynne, Nick Grosso, Judy Upton, Meredith Oakes, Sarah Kane, Anthony Neilson, Judith Johnson, James Stock, Jez Butterworth, Marina Carr, Phyllis Nagy, Simon Block, Martin McDonagh, Mark Ravenhill, Ayub Khan Din, Tamantha Hammerschlag, Jess Walters, Ché Walker, Conor McPherson,

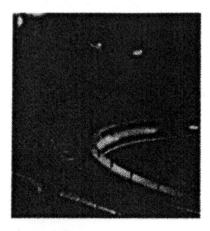

photo: Andy Chopping

Simon Stephens, Richard Bean, Roy Williams, Gary Mitchell, Mick Mahoney, Rebecca Gilman, Christopher Shinn, Kia Corthron, David Gieselmann, Marius von Mayenburg, David Eldridge, Leo Butler, Zinnie Harris, Grae Cleugh, Roland Schimmelpfennig, DeObia Oparei, Vassily Sigarev, the Presnyakov Brothers and Lucy Prebble. This expanded programme of new plays has been made possible through the support of A.SK Theater Projects and the Skirball Foundation, The Jerwood Charity, the American Friends of the Royal Court Theatre and many in association with the Royal National Theatre Studio.

In recent years there have been record-breaking productions at the box office, with capacity houses for Roy Williams' Fallout, Terry Johnson's Hitchcock Blonde, Caryl Churchill's A Number, Jez Butterworth's The Night Heron, Rebecca Gilman's Boy Gets Girl, Kevin Elyot's Mouth to Mouth, David Hare's My Zinc Bed and Conor McPherson's The Weir, which transferred to the West End in October 1998 and ran for nearly two years at the Duke of York's Theatre.

The newly refurbished theatre in Sloane Square opened in February 2000, with a policy still inspired by the first artistic director George Devine. The Royal Court is an international theatre for new plays and new playwrights, and the work shapes contemporary drama in Britain and overseas.

Douglas Hodge
Theatre includes: Three Sisters (ATG); The Winter's Tale (RSC), The Caretaker (Comedy); Betrayal, Pericles, King Lear, Blinded by the Sun (RNT); The Collection/The Lover (Donmar); No Mans Land, Moonlight, The Possibilities, Coriolanus (Almeida/Comedy); Romeo and Juliet (Birmingham Rep); Hamlet (Bolton Octagon); Twelfth Night (Young Vic); Norman Conquests (Nottingham Playhouse); A Midsummer Night's Dream (Regents Park Open Air).
As a director theatre includes: The Dumb Waiter and Other Pieces (Oxford Playhouse).
Television includes: Redcap, The Way We Live Now, The Russian Bride, The Law, Only Fools and Horses, A Scold's Bridle, It Could Be You, True Love, Men of the Month, Middlemarch, Bliss, Anglo Saxon Attitudes, A Fatal Inversion, Capital City, Open Fire.
Film includes: Vanity Fair, Saigon Baby, Hollow Reed, The Trail, Salome's Last Dance, Diamond Skulls.
As a director, film includes: Victoria Station, Forest People.

Terry Johnson (director)
For the Royal Court, as writer: Hitchcock Blonde, Hysteria, Cries from the Mammal House, Insignificance.
Other plays include, as writer: Cleo, Camping, Emmanuelle and Dick, Dead Funny (Hampstead/Vaudeville/West End tour); Imagine Drowning (Hampstead); Tuesday's Child (Theatre Royal, Stratford); Unsuitable for Adults; Amabel (Bush); Days Here So Dark (Paines Plough).
As director: The Graduate (Plymouth Theater/Broadway/Gielgud); Entertaining Mr Sloane (Arts); Sparkleshark (RNT); The Memory of Water (Hampstead/Vaudeville); Elton John's Glasses (Palace Theatre, Watford); Cracked (Hampstead); The Libertine (Steppenwolf, Chicago); Just Between Ourselves, Ragdoll (Bristol Old Vic); Death of a Salesman (Theatre Royal, York).
Television includes: Cor Blimey!, The Bite, The Lorelei, Way Upstream.

Claire Lovett (assistant director)
Theatre includes: Oleanna (Garrick); A Doll's House (Southwark Playhouse); Dirty Butterfly (Soho).

Anna Maxwell Martin
Theatre includes: His Dark Materials, Three Sisters, Honour, Coast of Utopia (RNT); Little Foxes (Donmar).
Television includes: Midsomer Murders, North and South.
Film includes: Enduring Love.

Bruno Poet (lighting designer)
Theatre includes: Volpone, Major Barbara, Playboy of the Western World, Cold Meat Party & The Seagull, Les Blancs, The Homecoming (Royal Exchange); Alice in Wonderland (Bristol Old Vic); Don Juan (Lyric, Hammersmith); The Skin of Our Teeth (Young Vic); Midnight's Children (RSC Barbican, Michigan & New York); Antarctica (Savoy); The Birthday Party, Sexual Perversity in Chicago, The Shawl (Sheffield Crucible); King Lear (ETT/Old Vic); Just Between Ourselves, The External, So Long life (Bath/No 1 Tours); Twelfth Night, Loves Labours Lost, The Cherry Orchard, The Taming of the Shrew, (ETT); Peter Pan, Twelfth Night, The Duchess of Malfi (Dundee Rep); Things You Shouldn't Say Past Midnight (Soho Theatre); Neville's Island (Watford Palace); Royal Supreme, Musik (Plymouth Theatre Royal).
Opera includes: seven consecutive seasons for Garsington Opera and Don Giovanni (Opera North); Rusalka, Manon (Opera North); The Magic Flute (Scottish Opera); Girl of Sand (Almeida Opera); Arabella and Fidelio (De Vlaamse Opera); The Marriage of Figaro, Orpheus in the Underworld (GEH); La Traviata, Fidelio (English Touring Opera); Berlin to Broadway (Denmark); Orfeo et Euridice (Opera National du Rhin); The Turn of the Screw (Brighton Festival); Ottone (Royal College of Music); Norma (Gran Teatro del Liceu Barcelona).

AWARDS FOR ROYAL COURT

Jez Butterworth won the 1995 George Devine Award, the Writers' Guild New Writer of the Year Award, the Evening Standard Award for Most Promising Playwright and the Olivier Award for Best Comedy for Mojo.

The Royal Court was the overall winner of the 1995 Prudential Award for the Arts for creativity, excellence, innovation and accessibility. The Royal Court Theatre Upstairs won the 1995 Peter Brook Empty Space Award for innovation and excellence in theatre.

Michael Wynne won the 1996 Meyer-Whitworth Award for The Knocky. Martin McDonagh won the 1996 George Devine Award, the 1996 Writers' Guild Best Fringe Play Award, the 1996 Critics' Circle Award and the 1996 Evening Standard Award for Most Promising Playwright for The Beauty Queen of Leenane. Marina Carr won the 19th Susan Smith Blackburn Prize (1996/7) for Portia Coughlan. Conor McPherson won the 1997 George Devine Award, the 1997 Critics' Circle Award and the 1997 Evening Standard Award for Most Promising Playwright for The Weir. Ayub Khan Din won the 1997 Writers' Guild Awards for Best West End Play and Writers' Guild New Writer of the Year and the 1996 John Whiting Award for East is East (co-production with Tamasha).

At the 1998 Tony Awards, Martin McDonagh's The Beauty Queen of Leenane (co-production with Druid Theatre Company) won four awards including Garry Hynes for Best Director and was nominated for a further two. Eugene Ionesco's The Chairs (co-production with Theatre de Complicite) was nominated for six Tony awards. David Hare won the 1998 Time Out Live Award for Outstanding Achievement and six awards in New York including the Drama League, Drama Desk and New York Critics Circle Award for Via Dolorosa. Sarah Kane won the 1998 Arts Foundation Fellowship in Playwriting. Rebecca Prichard won the 1998 Critics' Circle Award for Most Promising Playwright for Yard Gal (co-production with Clean Break).

Conor McPherson won the 1999 Olivier Award for Best New Play for The Weir. The Royal Court won the 1999 ITI Award for Excellence in International Theatre. Sarah Kane's Cleansed was judged Best Foreign Language Play in 1999 by Theater Heute in Germany. Gary Mitchell won the 1999 Pearson Best Play Award for Trust. Rebecca Gilman was joint winner of the 1999 George Devine Award and won the 1999 Evening Standard Award for Most Promising Playwright for The Glory of Living.

In 1999, the Royal Court won the European theatre prize New Theatrical Realities, presented at Taormina Arte in Sicily, for its efforts in recent years in discovering and producing the work of young British dramatists.

Roy Williams and Gary Mitchell were joint winners of the George Devine Award 2000 for Most Promising Playwright for Lift Off and The Force of Change respectively. At the Barclays Theatre Awards 2000 presented by the TMA, Richard Wilson won the Best Director Award for David Gieselmann's Mr Kolpert and Jeremy Herbert won the Best Designer Award for Sarah Kane's 4.48 Psychosis. Gary Mitchell won the Evening Standard's Charles Wintour Award 2000 for Most Promising Playwright for The Force of Change. Stephen Jeffreys' I Just Stopped by to See the Man won an AT&T: On Stage Award 2000.

David Eldridge's Under the Blue Sky won the Time Out Live Award 2001 for Best New Play in the West End. Leo Butler won the George Devine Award 2001 for Most Promising Playwright for Redundant. Roy Williams won the Evening Standard's Charles Wintour Award 2001 for Most Promising Playwright for Clubland. Grae Cleugh won the 2001 Olivier Award for Most Promising Playwright for Fucking Games. Richard Bean was joint winner of the George Devine Award 2002 for Most Promising Playwright for Under the Whaleback. Caryl Churchill won the 2002 Evening Standard Award for Best New Play for A Number. Vassily Sigarev won the 2002 Evening Standard Charles Wintour Award for Most Promising Playwright for Plasticine. Ian MacNeil won the 2002 Evening Standard Award for Best Design for A Number and Plasticine. Peter Gill won the 2002 Critics' Circle Award for Best New Play for The York Realist (English Touring Theatre). Ché Walker won the 2003 George Devine Award for Most Promising Playwright for Flesh Wound. Lucy Prebble won the 2003 Critics' Circle Award and the 2004 George Devine Award for Most Promising Playwright for The Sugar Syndrome.

ROYAL COURT BOOKSHOP

The Royal Court bookshop offers a diverse selection of contemporary plays and publications on the theory and practice of modern drama. The staff specialise in assisting with the selection of audition monologues and scenes.
Royal Court playtexts from past and present productions cost £2.
The Bookshop is situated in the downstairs ROYAL COURT BAR AND FOOD.
Monday–Friday 3–10pm, Saturday 2–10pm
For information tel: 020 7565 5024
or email: bookshop@royalcourttheatre.com

PROGRAMME SUPPORTERS

The Royal Court (English Stage Company Ltd) receives its principal funding from Arts Council England, London. It is also supported financially by a wide range of private companies and public bodies and earns the remainder of its income from the box office and its own trading activities. The Royal Borough of Kensington & Chelsea gives an annual grant to the Royal Court Young Writers Programme.
The Genesis Foundation supports the International Season and Young Writers Festival.

The Jerwood Charity supports new plays by new playwrights through the Jerwood New Playwrights series. The Skirball Foundation funds a Playwrights' Programme at the theatre. The Artistic Director's Chair is supported by a lead grant from The Peter Jay Sharp Foundation, contributing to the activities of the Artistic Director's office. Bloomberg Mondays, the Royal Court's reduced price ticket scheme, is supported by Bloomberg. Over the past eight years the BBC has supported the Gerald Chapman Fund for directors.

ROYAL COURT
SLOANE SQUARE

Jerwood Theatre Downstairs

28 October - 4 December
FORTY WINKS
by **Kevin Elyot**

Director *Katie Mitchell*
Designer *Hildegard Bechtler*
Lighting *Paule Constable*
Sound *Ian Dickinson*
Cast includes: *Anastasia Hille, Stephen Kennedy, Paul Ready, Dominic Rowan.*

Jerwood Theatre Upstairs

YOUNG PLAYWRIGHTS' SEASON 2004
A Genesis Project

9 - 25 September
BONE
by John Donnelly

1 - 30 October
THE WEATHER
by Clare Pollard

5 - 16 October
BEAR HUG
by Robin French

5 - 20 November
FRESH KILLS
by Elyzabeth Gregory Wilder

26 November - 18 December
A GIRL IN A CAR WITH A MAN
by Rob Evans

BOX OFFICE
020 7565 5000
BOOK ONLINE
www.royalcourttheatre.com

Dumb Show

For the McLaughlins, in memory of Bill

'Ignorance is strength.'

– George Orwell

Characters

Barry
Liz
Greg

Act One

Scene One

Five-star hotel room.

Barry *is wearing an immaculate suit.*
Greg *is holding a bottle of champagne.*
Liz *is carrying a laptop computer case.*
Liz *and* **Greg** *are wearing pinstripe.*

Barry   Barry. How you doing?

Liz   Hi, I'm Jane . . .

Greg   John . . .

Barry   Jane. John . . .

Greg   Jane. Barry . . .

Liz   Barry. John. Hi . . .

Greg   Excellent . . .

Barry *and* **Liz** *shake hands.*

Barry   Cor, that's a good handshake. She's got a grip like
a boa constrictor.

Liz   Oh, I'm a weakling really . . .

Barry *and* **Greg** *shake hands.*

Barry   Hello. You're not a mason. There was nothing
funny about your handshake. That was the classic chop
from the top. That was a classic money handshake. (*Does it.*)
'I'm going to dominate you and take all your money.' And
this is a showbiz handshake. (*Does it.*) 'You're not paying for
this, you want my soul, leave me alone.'

Greg   Very witty.

Liz   You must be tired.

Greg   Give that man a drink.

Liz   Give him a seat.

Greg   Give that man a cigar as they say.

Liz   You must be exhausted.

Barry   Oh – you know –

Liz   Exhausted.

Barry   Used to it really . . . you know . . .

He loosens his tie.

Greg   Loved the show.

Liz   Loved it.

Greg   You really sweat under those lights.

Barry   Do I smell . . . ?

Liz   You smell fine.

Barry   I'm a fright without my make-up.

Greg   You were brilliant.

Liz   Brilliant.

Greg   Brilliant.

They go to sit. They pause. He goes to sit. He pauses. They almost sit. Wait. They sit.

Sorry.

Liz   Sorry.

Barry   No, I'm –

Greg   Is this a good time?

Liz   Ruth said it was best to bring you here.

Barry   Usually the green room is the . . .

Liz   Oh, but you had all your friends . . .

Greg   We wanted somewhere nice and quiet so we could have you all to ourselves.

Liz   I'm such a big fan.

Greg   Huge fans. Very big fans indeed.

Liz   I've never been in a TV studio before.

Greg   That was hilarious.

Liz   I've never been in a 'green room'. It wasn't very green.

Greg   I laughed until I stopped.

Barry   Y . . . oh very good . . .

Greg   (You like that?)

Barry   (Very witty.)

Greg   O-ho, you've got competition.

Liz   Stop it, John. He's teasing. Really he's not very funny at all.

Greg   Ouch. Blimey. Say what you really think, Jane.

Liz   I really liked the stuff about your wife.

Greg   Lovely stuff. The wife gags. Classic. What is he like?

Barry   Well, you see my wedding anniversary was last week actually . . .   .

Greg   All good stuff. Have a little celebration? Take her out somewhere swank?

Barry   Took her to the Ivy.

Liz   It's all right for some.

Greg   And why not, sir?

Liz   It's all right for some, eh, John?

Greg   Why not, sir?

Barry Well, they're very good with names, you see. They're trained to remember Valerie's. If you buy smokes they're trained to unwrap them and put them on a little dish. They get you a car afterwards. You keep expecting somebody to come up and groom you for nits.

Liz What does Valerie do?

Barry She just looks blank and sort of lets it all wash over her.

Greg Classic! (See . . . ? He's just . . .)

Liz No, for a living. She still works, doesn't she?

Barry Absolutely, she's trying to breed ponies. It's not going very well. I think she's got a few duds. She's forever cleaning up after them. The stable's a pigsty . . .

Pause. They suddenly laugh.

Greg Classic! Oh, that's very good. Very, very good indeed. (Isn't he marvellous? This is what I was telling you about –)

Liz Brilliant, mm . . .

Greg (He's 'on' tonight.) Very, very funny. Very witty. Very astute. I like it a lot. You really know your stuff, Barry – seriously, that thing about chickens was just brilliant. It was brilliant.

Barry You liked the chicken gag?

Greg I am a sucker for chicken gags. Chicken gags kill me. Do the one about the genie and the bottle.

Liz Oh, that's such an old joke.

Greg An oldie but a goodie. That joke kills me.

Barry No – I don't want to kill you –

Greg Oh, go on. A drunk sees a genie in a bottle of brandy and the genie says, 'I'll give you three wishes . . .'

And the drunk has a drink and he looks at the bottle and he goes –

Barry   OK, yeah . . .

Greg   'I want a bottle that never empties . . .'

Barry   Yeah, I don't really . . .

Liz   OK, John . . .

Greg   And the genie – no, listen – the genie waves his magic wand and 'poof . . .' and there it is . . . bottle that never empties . . . The drunk drinks it down . . . it fills up again . . . and the genie says –

Liz   (John, please . . .)

Greg   'You've got two wishes left . . .' Hold on, and the drunk says . . . listen . . . the drunk says, 'I'll have another two of these.' (*He laughs.*)

Pause.

Barry   What's funny about it?

Greg   I just really like . . . I think it's a funny, a funny –

Barry   He's obviously a really sad individual. It's not funny any more.

Greg   It's just a bit of innocent fun . . .

Barry   It isn't innocent any more either. He's a drunk. He's got problems. What's funny about that? Why is it funny?

Greg   Bec . . . because . . . why is it funny, Jane?

Barry   I can remember when heart attacks were funny. In the seventies. Big sight gag. Until Tommy Cooper hopped the twig. Drunks used to be a scream – until Margaret Thatcher was elected – and began governing like one. The Irish: We used to laugh at Irishmen. Now they laugh at us. Jokes about religion stopped being funny after Nine/Eleven – jokes about fat people stop being funny after 7/Elevens and McDonald's. We're running out of things to laugh at, so now we laugh at things which aren't even funny, just to feel normal. We're living in a world of hollow laughter and forgive me for not joining in but quite frankly I preferred the real thing.

Pause.

Greg   Now you see now that's brilliant. Really.

Liz   That's deep.

Greg   Very deep.

Liz   The *insight*.

Greg   Very wise.

Liz   *Astute.* Mm . . .

Greg   You know, it's so nice to see somebody like yourself at the, you know, at the top of your game, at the pinnacle of your powers, as they say, it really is a privilege . . .

Liz   Absolutely a real privilege.

Liz *crosses her legs.*

Greg   Jane, will you please put your legs away please – what is she like – flashing her knickers all over the shop – she is so naughty . . .

Liz   Don't look then, John . . .

Greg   If you put the goods in the window . . .

Liz   Don't look then . . . nobody noticed . . .

Greg   Well, I think they did.

Liz   (Sorry. Office politics.)

Greg   It's Friday night.

Liz   And it's Friday night. 'Crazy-crazy-crazy.' Everybody has to be silly. It's compulsory.

Faint laughs.

Liz *starts unwrapping the foil from the champagne.*

Greg   Come on, Jane. Put your wrist into it. You've had enough practice . . .

Liz   Shut up, John . . .

Liz *massages the cork.*

Greg   That's right, massage its cork.

Liz   It's quite hard.

Greg   I'm quite hard now. Eh? Now we're talking. A nice '92. Now we are talking.

He produces three champagne glasses from the minibar.

Now we are speaking. All the trimmings . . .

Barry   No, actually – thanks all the same. Much as I'd love to.

Liz   Go on. Treat yourself.

Barry   Well, I – well . . .

He watches as she uncorks the bottle.

Liz   Ooh goodness!

Greg   Blimey, shake it up why don't you, Jane? Give it a big spurt. You can't help yourself.

Liz *pours and tries to hand* **Barry** *a glass of champagne but* **Barry** *waves it away.*

Barry   No no no no, not for me . . .

Liz   I've poured it now.

Barry   I'm fine. Thank you. Really. No . . . thank you . . .

Liz   Sure?

Liz *hands* **Greg** *a glass and chinks glasses and they drink and smack their lips.*

Greg   Oh, that's a good drop.

Liz   That's lovely.

Greg   That's a good drop.

Liz   That's very good.

Greg   That's a very good drop.

Liz   Fruity.

Greg   'A fruity, a fruity, a cheeky little number – cheeky but butch.' Eh?

Barry *watches them drink.*

Greg   Chin-chin.

Liz   Cheers.

They sit.

You sure I can't twist your arm?

Barry   You can twist anything you like, love, won't make any difference to me.

Greg (*handing over a glass, pouring*)   Oh go on. Why not, sir. Eh? That's what it's all about. (*Winks.*) Go on.

Barry *stares, hesitates. Then almost takes a sip but changes his mind and puts the glass down.* **Greg** *puts his glass down too, rubbing his hands together, brisk.*

Greg   Anyway. So. OK. I expect Ruth filled you in . . .

Barry   She mentioned she had an account.

Greg   OK.

Barry   She said everybody had accounts. Everybody upstairs. One of the writers. I never talk to the writers. It only encourages them . . .

Liz   Ruth thought you'd be keen . . .

Barry   I adore Ruth. Really. She's smart, she's funny, she's sexy – in a kind of bluestocking, slightly mumsy type of way. I'll tell you something else. She has fought tooth and

claw to get the series into the shape it's in. Loyal, you see.
Loyalty goes a long way with me.

Liz   She mentioned you weren't entirely happy with
certain things . . .

Greg   Certain arrangements . . .

Barry   I told them, I said, 'You pay chicken feed, you get
monkeys.' Ruth knows. She's on to it. She won't let me
down. You see, we go back a long way Ruth and I . . .

Greg   Well, you see, we'd take you on just on the basis of
what you're going to earn in your retirement –

Liz   In residuals –

Greg   In residuals, absolutely.

Barry   I have no end of trouble with banks. It's impossible
to speak to anyone. You can't ring up, everything's menu
this, password that, it's like ringing MI5 . . .

Greg   You're not getting the right kind of service.

Barry   Well, quite frankly, at this point in my career, with
my –

Liz   With your earning power.

Barry   Precisely. I tend to expect –

Greg   You don't belong on the high street.

Barry   You know, I really feel I don't . . .

Greg   Nothing wrong with the high street if you're a wage
monkey, they provide an efficient, perfectly satisfactory
service for your average working person –

Barry   Sure, if you're just an average stiff –

Greg   But the thing is this, Barry: if you own a Roller you
don't go to a back-street mechanic. D'you follow what I
mean? You don't just call the AA. You go first class.

Barry   Or at the very least business . . .

Liz (*simultaneous with 'business'*)   Business . . .

Greg   You pick up the phone and you speak to me.

Barry   Well, that's what I want. I want to speak to a human being.

Greg   You pick up the phone and you speak to me. That's all.

Barry   OK . . . nobody else?

Greg   Nope. Just me. Or Jane here if I'm not at my desk or on another call. Any time of the day, anywhere in the world. Which I should imagine is especially useful to somebody like yourself in your line of work . . . I can also arrange traveller's cheques, foreign currency, a new mortgage –

Liz   We can get you a great mortgage.

Greg   Have you got a mortgage?

Barry   I have – yes – but –

Greg   What sort of mortgage?

Barry   Oh – it's not a very good one –

Greg   We should take a look at it –

Barry   Well – OK –

Greg   Whatever – wherever you are, whenever, I take care of everything.

Barry   You . . . ?

Greg   I take care of everything. Has Ruth talked to you about the talk?

Pause.

Barry   A . . . what do you mean? What talk?

Greg   You don't know about this? (Why doesn't he know about this?)

Liz   We were going to ask you to come and do a talk at the bank. Nothing freaky. Just come and talk.

Barry   Just . . . talk to . . . some . . . who?

Greg   Everybody. Staff. A few selected clients. We'll have a dinner.

Liz   And after dinner you could do your talk. Totally informal. They'll love it.

Greg   Totally informal. Exactly. The exact opposite of, of formal . . .

Liz   And fun. We want people to have fun.

Greg   You see, everybody has the idea it's no fun where we work. They think it's soulless. Far from it. Private banking is fun. Investment banking is a lot of fun as well. And what's more, it's very *lucrative.* Which is also, obviously, a whole lot of fun too . . . And that's where, you know, that's where you come into it.

Barry   I – ?

Greg   Because you're a very important person now, Barry, I don't know if you realise . . .

Liz   A very important client, Barry, if it all goes –

Greg   If this works out, yes, we would really value your account and, if I may say, the pleasure of your company, good sir.

Pause.

Barry   Well, OK. W . . . what would you want me to talk about?

Liz   What do you want to talk about?

Barry   I don't want to talk about anything, it was your idea.

Greg   Talk about the new series. Your experiences. Your views. I can imagine you can be quite, you know, quite 'controversial' when you put your mind to it and we'd actually welcome that.

Liz   Nothing wrong with a bit of controversy . . .

Greg   Controversy is crucial . . .

Liz   Crucial.

Greg   Tell it like it is.

Liz   We can show people a side of you they haven't seen before.

Barry   There isn't a side of me they haven't seen before, love. Ask Ruth. I'm what they call 'well documented'.

Greg   There will be a fee of course.

Barry   You can't 'buy' me. (*Snorts.*) What sort of fee are we talking about?

Greg   Well. A substantial fee . . .

Barry   How substantial?

Greg   A very substantial fee, Barry. A very 'substantial financial' as we say in the trade.

Barry   O-ho. 'Very substantial', eh? How substantial?

Greg *nods to* **Liz** *who takes out a card from the case and writes on it.*

Greg   This is how much we've got in the kitty. For corporate hospitality. Wining and dining. (*Pause.* **Barry** *stares.*) Yee see, you're a very clever man. I don't know if you're aware of it. But I think people could really learn from you – and have a laugh while they do it.

Barry *stares at the card again.*

Barry   W . . . I don't often come up to town, that's all. It's only when I'm taping shows.

Greg Pick a day, any day. We'll get you back, we'll book you in here, nice bit of lunch in the room with Jane – do what you have to do – go and do the talk in the evening.

Liz You should see the room service here. Steaks like telephone books.

Barry Y – I don't need feeding, love. I'm hardly a starving waif.

Greg You can come up here and she'll talk you through it, nothing to be nervous about.

Liz It would mean a lot to us . . .

Greg Barry, I'm not 'blowing smoke up your arse'.

Barry I would have noticed . . .

Faint laughs.

Greg Look. We're serious about this. Talk to your agent.

Barry Well, no, no, you know, there's no need for him to know about this just at the moment . . .

Liz But if it makes it easier . . .

Barry No, well, you see, he won't want a commission for this, you see. It's too much paper work. I don't mind giving him ten per cent when he's earned it . . . but then there's the VAT . . . paying *his* VAT on *his* commission is taking the piss a bit . . . then there's VAT on paperwork – I have to pay a bookkeeper and an accountant – they all charge VAT –

Greg The thing is, Barry, you're a bit of a 'national treasure' as they say . . .

Liz And it's about time people remembered that . . .

Barry Well, it's very nice of you to . . . uh . . . realise that . . . uh . . . could I just . . . ? (*Pause. Almost drinks but stops, puts glass down.*) Perhaps if I take a . . . ? Give me your number and I'll . . . (*Flips card over.*) Oh, I see it's . . . OK . . . (*Flips, stares.*) (I don't suppose it could do any . . .) Why not?

Greg *puts* **Barry**'s *glass in* **Barry**'s *hand.*

Greg   Why not indeed?

Greg *drinks.*
Liz *drinks.*
Barry *stares.*

Blackout.

Scene Two

Liz *is in a sexy dress, examining herself in the mirror. She rearranges her clothes, her hair, applies lipstick.*

Barry *is rummaging in the minibar, examining miniature bottles.*

Barry   Dogs believe in heaven and hell and cats don't. Dogs believe in everything. They're not choosy. They're man's best friend. Dogs are morally superior to cats but cats have a better sense of irony. It's obvious. When a dog does something wrong – chases a cat up a tree, savages a small child and so on and so forth – you say, 'Bad dog,' and the dog panics and puts his tail between his legs and looks all guilty. He's going, 'Oh no. What have I done? It wasn't me.' They feel terrible. They get so embarrassed. When a cat does something wrong – you leave a piece of fish out of the fridge, the cat chews the fish, the cat scratches the baby, you scold the cat, he just looks at you like you're stupid. 'Don't look at *me, you* left it there.' It's written all over their faces. They don't care. You say, 'I'm gonna kill you,' and they're going, 'I don't care, I'm a cat, I've got nine lives. Fuck you.' (*Gestures, V-sign.*)

Liz   Excellent, no, yeah, that's really good . . .

Liz *places the computer case on the table and positions it carefully as they talk.*

Barry   Is that the sort of . . . ? (*Gestures.*)

Liz   Yeah, no, yeah, that's, you know . . .

Barry   OK . . .

Liz   If you did away with the, the routine and the, you know, the jokes and just talked, just chatted, about your life, your philosophies . . . the ups and downs . . . yeah? You see? It's more truthful. More authentic.

Barry   Do away with the jokes?

Liz   Tell your story. Tell us something we don't know . . .

Barry   The whole point about jokes is they're just jokes. They're not true stories. The whole point about why the chicken crossed the road is that A) we don't know the chicken personally and so B) who cares? It's a chicken. Chickens are funny. They just are.

Liz   But we still want to know why it crossed the road. What's its, you know, background?

Barry   It's a chicken. It'll be lunch soon. That's its background. A horse walks into a bar and the barman says, 'Why the long face?' It's funny because it's a horse. Not because the horse may or may not be alcohol-dependent . . .

Liz   It's funny because it's *true* . . .

Barry   It's funny because it's funny. It isn't remotely true. Why is a horse in a bar true?

Liz   Bec . . . because horses really do have long faces. They do! (**Barry** *stares.*) If you said, 'A, a, a *monkey* walks into a bar and the barman says, "Why the long face?"' it wouldn't be funny because monkeys have hairy faces . . .

Barry   They also have extremely long arms and opposing thumbs but if you said, 'A monkey walks into a bar and the barman says, "Why the extremely long arms and opposing thumbs?"' they wouldn't laugh if their lives depended on it.

Eh? You're a, sorry, love, but you work in a bank. Leave it to the experts.

Liz   OK . . . I was only saying . . .

Barry   D'you know what I mean?

Liz   Sure – no – yeah. No. Let's push on, shall we? I'd really like to nail it before dinner . . .

Barry *pours a brandy, sips.*

Liz   Have another brandy . . . yes . . . that's really helpful . . .

Barry   Would you possibly be able to make it out to cash? My fee. Will you be able to, to – ?

Liz   I'll talk to John. Absolutely. It'll go straight into your new account.

Barry   But give it to me first . . .

Liz   Eh?

Barry   Give it to me first . . .

Liz   OK. I'll give you the cheque and you can put it in an envelope and send it to John.

Barry   Yes, but – you see – cash would be better . . .

Liz   He'll organise the cash. Don't worry about any of it . . .

Barry   It's just the VAT thing . . .

Liz   I'll sort it out.

Barry   If I could trust my bank not to *lose* it . . .

Liz   I'll make a note of it.

Barry   No, but you see they could *lose* the cheque. This always happens when you change banks. They say it went to the new bank, the new bank swears it went to the old bank. They're such bullshitters . . . present company excepted . . .

Barry *tops up his brandy and sips.*

Liz   You might want to slow down a bit actually –

Barry   O-ho. I want to speed up –

Liz   All the same, Barry, there's plenty of time to, you know . . . there's a lot to get through . . .

Barry (*refills the tumbler, sips*)   'Behind the scenes' and all that shit.

Liz   Sorry?

Barry   'Behind the scenes.' You want me to talk about the show. Behind the glamour . . . the reality . . . the banality . . . all that crap.

Liz   Well, if that's –

Barry   'The crap behind the crap: a show made by idiots, for idiots . . . because of idiots.' I don't want to talk about it. It's a waste of time. (*Lights a cigarette.*)

Liz   OK. Uh. Fine . . .

Barry   I get letters all the time. 'Dear Barry, I want to be on TV. Help me.' You know. The proles . . . they send me Polaroids with their tits out. 'I'm very nice. About five three. Forty-five years old. I can *juggle*. I will give you a blow job.' They're always some sort of cripple or, you know, always deformed in some appalling way or another . . . speccy . . . they can never spell. Terrible handwriting. They come to my dressing room after the show and just hang about, staring, utterly blank, waiting to be blessed, waiting for the laying on of hands. (*He mimics open-mouthed blank stares.*) Like the victims of some sort of terrible natural disaster. (*He mimics again.*) Lobotomised. Like they're catching flies. They're wankers.

Pause.

Liz   I suppose it can't be easy . . .

Barry   Well, I'd miss them if they weren't there obviously . . .

Liz   And they'd miss you, I think . . .

Barry   Well, it's not my problem. Fuck 'em. D'you know what I really wanted to be before all this? I wanted to be a schoolteacher. Something which enabled me to use my *brain*, Jane. To, you know, 'give something back'. You see? Pass on my knowledge. There is no greater gift. My mum used to say, 'You've got a good brain, use it.' She wanted me to be a teacher. Nurses and teachers are the real people. They're the ones who count. I should have been a fucking headmaster or just, you know, just, worked with animals or something. (*Belches, sips.*)

Pause.

Liz   You don't seem very, if you don't mind me . . . you don't seem very happy, at the moment, I must say . . .

Pause.

Barry (*stares*)   Y . . . well . . . no . . . no, not so happy lately, I suppose, in some ways . . . just . . . you know . . .

Liz   Do you want to . . . you know . . . talk about it? (*Gestures.*)

Barry   Well, I, well, there's nothing to . . . really . . . (*Pause.*) Uh . . . I work too hard, you see. Lots of travelling, you see, when I'm on tour. Sometimes I have to come up to London to tape the show . . . do publicity . . . I haven't been home in . . . I'm always in some shitty hotel, you know, the Ramada, the Holiday Inn, washing with, you know, those tiny soap bars, shampooing with tiny shampoo bottles, drinking out of miniatures – who designs those places? Midgets? People with tiny hands like monkeys? They're so stingy. In the not too distant future, they won't even give you soap. You'll have to give *them* soap. You'll check in at reception, you'll hand over your credit card, a bar of soap and a bowl of fruit and only then will they give you the key.

You'll go up to your room, you'll have to make your own
bed, then you'll have to find the maid and make her bed.
The air conditioner never goes off, there's no extractor fan
in the bathroom so the room always smells vaguely of warm
shit . . . it's probably not even mine. Probably wafts in from
the air conditioning. It's somebody else's, recycled. I just
want to go home. I never see my kids
. . . I miss my family . . .

Liz   I can see they're very important to you. I can see
Valerie's obviously very, you know, good for you . . .

Barry   W . . . y . . . n . . .

Liz   Oh . . . she is . . . I'm sure she is . . . isn't she?

Barry   Well . . .

Liz   Yeah – no – it's none of my business obviously, I
didn't mean to, to pry.

Silence.

Barry   You see, my mother died a few months ago. That's
probably where this all . . . it's the one thing I couldn't
handle really, death. (*Pause.*) She was lovely, my mum. She
was a nurse at Cromwell Hospital. I adore nurses. I feel safe
with nurses. Never had a harsh word for anybody. She
taught me to always try to see the best in people. 'Never let
the sun go down on an argument,' she used to say. 'Always
give people the benefit of the doubt.' Erm . . . 'Never
mistrust your friends.' 'If you can't do a good turn never do
a bad turn.' What a load of old balls. Different generation,
see. Wartime. The Blitz. 'Never let the sun go down on an
argument because you don't know what could happen in the
night.' Could wake up dead. Then you'd be sorry. (*Pause.*)
No, you see, it's not that I'm unhappy. I'm just . . . I'm
sensitive. Yes. And just generally probably, you know . . . a
bit of a mummy's boy really, I suppose, and so now . . . I'm
a bit of a . . . I'm a, a complicated guy . . .

Liz   A 'mass of contradictions'.

Barry   Well, no, I'm just weak and easily confused and I always need to be the centre of attention, that's all . . . I need the, you know, the love of an audience. Which is pathetic. I know. It's –

Liz   No . . . not at all . . .

Barry   On the other hand . . .

Liz   What's wrong with that?

Barry   My point exactly. And there's nothing wrong with that. What's wrong with that? It's a good living. (*Pause.*) But, you see, then I meet somebody like yourself and I . . . see, I yearn for normality. Dullness, even.

Liz   Thank you very much . . .

Barry   No, I yearn to have . . . what you have. You're a, a, a lovely, straightforward, *lovely*, *ordinary* young woman . . . there's no side to you, no *pretence* . . .

Liz   I don't know. I am a bit dull, really, it's probably true . . .

Barry   No. Not at all. You're just . . .

Liz   A bit plain . . .

Barry   Not at all . . .

Liz   'Plain Jane.'

Barry   I think plain women are marvellous. You know where you stand with plain women. It's what's inside that gets me going.

Liz   I'm pretty uninteresting on the inside too . . .

Barry   No no no no no – not in the least.

Liz   Oh . . .

Barry   No.

Liz   Yeah.

Barry   No! I think you're . . . you know . . .

Liz   S . . . sometimes I worry I'm actually a bit, you know, boring sometimes.

Barry   Oh no. 'Boring.' Heaven forbid. The worst thing in the entire world . . .

Liz   I think John thinks I'm boring . . .

Barry   Well, I think he's boring . . .

Liz   He just sometimes gives me this look, he just looks at me very, I don't know, boredly. Just because I'm not some kind of grinning, whippet-thin, bleached Barbie-doll-type woman like everybody else in finance, I expect . . .

Barry   You look OK to me . . .

Liz   Because of course he's addicted to porn . . .

Barry (*beat*)   Uh-huh . . .

Liz   It's always on his laptop. I don't mind a bit of porn, everybody likes porn . . .

Barry   Y . . . in small doses . . .

Liz   I can look at, you know, I look at women's bodies sometimes . . .

Barry   I'm the same . . .

Liz   Everybody has, you know, fantasies . . .

Barry   Nothing wrong with fantasy . . .

Liz   But you know, within reason . . . !

Barry   You have to draw the line somewhere . . .

Liz   . . . You have to be sensible about it . . . all these melon-breasted, tiny-waisted women, shaved to within an inch of their lives, lolling about with their mouths open. It's all so fake and phoney . . .

Barry   It's not realistic . . .

Liz Women have hair!

Barry I adore hairy women . . .

Liz I've got a moustache . . .

Barry I like moustaches on women . . .

Liz Stop me if I'm, you know, going on a bit. I can be quite, you know, quite 'outspoken' . . .

Barry 'Tell it like it is.' Outspokenness is, you know . . . (*Pause.*) Are you, uh, married, Jane?

Liz Jesus Christ, no . . .

Barry Have you . . . uh . . . have you got a boyfriend?

Liz Not at the moment . . .

Barry Why haven't you got a boyfriend?

Liz Nobody has boyfriends any more . . .

Barry Why not?

Liz I don't know. None of my girlfriends have boyfriends . . . it's just normal, I think . . .

Barry Is it? Why?

Liz Well, it's just . . .

Barry When was the last time you had a boyfriend?

Liz I don't know . . . two years ago . . .

Barry Two years ago! That's ridiculous. You need to get a boyfriend. Boyfriends are fun.

Liz It never really works out . . .

Barry I don't believe you . . .

Liz It's, uh, you don't want to hear all this . . . and I don't really want to tell you, so . . .

Barry Go on. I'm listening.

Liz   No, it's all bollocks . . .

Barry   Spit it out! Tell your Uncle Barry . . .

Liz   It seems to be getting harder to get to know people. Maybe it's just getting harder to 'want' to know people. (I say 'people', I probably mean 'men' . . .)

Barry   (You know *me*.)

Liz   It's not as if I have high expectations – I don't – I have really low expectations . . . I just think men don't like me because I'm, you know, I'm quite hard work, I suppose . . .

Barry   I like you . . .

Liz   I talk too much, I know . . .

Barry   I like talking to you . . .

He looks her in the eye.
A 'moment'.
Silence.
She fidgets with the case.

Liz   . . . Anyway . . . perhaps you should have some water now. You really are pretty . . . getting quite . . .

Barry   What? Getting what?

Liz   All those little bottles . . .

Barry   What have I done?

Liz   You're just, you know, you've become very . . . you're drinking quite a lot now . . . I don't mind . . . you can drink as much as you like . . . I just don't want to encourage you to –

Barry   O-ho! I love a drink. I got drunk on my nan's sherry when I was five years old. I thought it was Ribena. When I got it in my mouth, cor! Rocket fuel. I nearly blasted off. I was doing backflips before I could do, you know, somersaults. And so, you see, after that I wanted to try everything. And then I got a taste for . . . I got a taste for everything. (*Pause.*) People think it's this great truth serum, in actual fact it makes you *lie*. Makes you say things you've never said before, think things you've never thought before. Not because you've repressed them but because they've never even *occurred* to you. You see, human beings, Janie, need an alternate reality like a whale needs a blowhole. We need things to appear differently to what they really are or else we go insane. We're not interested in reality. We're interested in distorting it. Because it's the only way we can bear to be human. It's the only way we can bear this ONSLAUGHT . . . of death and loss and disaster . . . and the joy, you see, the joy . . . of birth . . . new life . . . love . . . sex? Eh? Sex is God's way of saying 'sorry'. It's compensation for growing up. But, you see, it confuses us. All this joy and then the 'paradox', see, when you kick the bucket.

Pause.

Liz   Wow, that's . . . no, yeah . . . I love the way you really just, you know, you don't give a fuck what people think about you . . .

Barry   Well, you see, it's a talent. It takes practice.

Liz   I don't think you need to practise. You're a natural.

Barry   O-ho. You should see me when I'm coked up to the eyeballs.

Liz   I've never even tried it . . .

Barry   You've never tried sherbet? Never? In your line of work . . . ?

Liz   Not so much in private banking . . .

Barry   Truly?

Liz   You're thinking of corporate banking . . .

Barry   Speed? Amphetamines?

Liz   I've led a rather sheltered existence . . .

Barry   You've never been curious? When I was a kid you could have a haircut, go to the flicks and buy a bag of amphetamine sulphate for a couple of bob and still have change for Liquorice Allsorts.

Liz   You sound like an expert.

Barry   I dabbled. I'll put my hand up to that.

Liz   Aha.

Barry   I dabbled every night. Gassed. Zipped. Ripped. Spaced. Fried like bacon and eggs. Wired to within an inch of my life . . .

Liz   I've tried slimming pills . . .

Barry   Coupla slimming pills and a pint of IPA, you'll think you're Spiderman. Pills. Powder. Uppers. Downers. Leapers. Bombers. Blues. Speed's marvellous! (Obviously you have to, uh, be a bit sensible about it. It messes with your mind a bit . . .)

He pours another brandy. Drinks.

Liz   Have you got any?

Barry   'Have I got any?' Priceless.

Liz   Have you? Show me.

Barry   OK, listen. Jane, Janie, you're a sweet girl, I appreciate that this is probably all very interesting to you but the thing is . . . I've obviously given you slightly the wrong impression here . . .

Liz   I like how you call me, Janie.

Pause.

Barry   W . . . ?

Liz   (*crossing her legs*)   Friendly . . . 'Janie'. Maybe this is something you should address in your speech.

Barry Eh?

Liz Your speech tonight . . .

Barry What's wrong with my speech? Am I slurring?

Liz No, I meant the past, the old, you know, habits . . .

Barry You mean . . . make it a bit more, you know,
'confessional' perhaps, and all that?

Liz If you want to. You might find it, you know, cathartic.

Barry I might find it addictive. (*Fishing in his pocket.*)

*He produces from his pockets a wrap of powder and tosses it on to the
table in front of them.*

Barry Here you go. Go on. Have some of that. Go on,
you're all right. Dig in.

Liz Oh . . . goodness me . . .

Barry It's not much but it'll give you a bump. Go on. Do
it on the cistern in the bathroom. It's a flat cistern . . .

Liz Goodness gracious . . . you're so naughty . . . 'Mad,
bad and dangerous to know.'

Barry O-ho. I used to be mad, bad and dangerous to
know. Now I'm just mad, bad, sad and a dad.

Liz Well, you really must've been, I think . . . !

Liz *places her hand on the case, moves it slightly.*
Barry *sits and rubs powder into his gums.*

Barry It's good stuff. Not rubbish. *Zippy.*

Liz Well, we have got a long day ahead of us . . .

Barry I'll get you some for later. How much d'you want?
Half a gram? I can be on that phone and it'll be here in five
minutes.

He drains his drink and picks up the phone.

Liz Actually, no. Please, really, no, I couldn't . . .

Barry   Go on. Take hard drugs with me. Rub it into your gums.

Liz   Blimey . . . no . . . oh . . .

Barry   Go on. It's nice. Tingly.

Liz   Put it away . . . God . . . what are you like?

She checks her watch.
He puts phone down.
He puts powder away.
He fidgets, taps his foot.
He drums on the table.
He stares.

OK . . . so . . .

Barry   What are you looking at me like that for?

Liz   Like what?

Barry   Like . . . funny . . .

Liz   I'm not.

Barry   What have I . . . ? You seem distant all of a sudden.

He lights a cigarette.
He gets up, wanders a bit.

Liz   I really ought to be making a move actually –

Barry   W. . . what about our grub?

Liz   Perhaps you could call up for a, a, a . . .

Barry   You must eat something . . .

Liz   Sandwich . . .

Barry   A sandwich? No. (*Staring.*) Look at you, you're all . . . you're so skinny . . . you're all legs and arms and eyes like . . . electromagnets . . . (*He grabs her elbow.*) Eh? Look at this . . .

Liz   No . . .

Barry (*tickling her*)   Eh? You're like a little bird!

Liz   I'm all right really. Thank you. I have to go now . . .

Barry (*clutching at her hand*)   No, don't let go – hold on –
just touch – (*Touches her hand to his face.*)

Liz   Barry . . .

Barry   No, just – touch . . . I haven't been touched by a
woman since I went to the dentist . . . (*A hand around her
waist.*)

Liz   What are you – ?

Barry   My wife, you see – my Valerie – she's very – she's
not very –

Liz   What are you do – ?

Barry   Just hold . . . hold me . . .

Liz   Doing?

Barry (*drawing her close*)   You see, I've been very –

Liz   Just –

Barry   Just –

Liz   Just –

Barry   I'm *lonely* . . .

Liz (*drawing away*)   I said *NO*.

Silence.

Barry   But that's enough about me. Who are you?

Blackout.

Scene Three

Barry is standing around, doing up his tie, checking his appearance in the mirror, stretching, etc.
Liz is pouring coffee.
Greg is in shirtsleeves.

Barry   Right. I'm hot to trot.

Greg   Well, all right then.

Barry   Locked and loaded.

Greg   Great.

Barry   Let's get ready to rumble.

Greg   OK, great . . .

Barry   Let's go. Where is it? On the Strand?

Liz   Coffee?

Barry   (Please . . .) How do we get there? I usually have a car . . .

Liz   How do you have it?

Barry   (Black no sugar – actually white – I'll flip my lid.)

He bounces on the balls of his feet.

It's just like doing stand-up . . .

He clears his throat, 'la-las' a scale.

I am an expert craftsman of the witty bon mot and a master philosopher. I'm a smooth-talking, fast-walking, fire-stoking, heavy-smoking, straight-shooting, heavy-hitting, side-splitting motherfucking hunka-hunka ramalama ding-dong, baby. And I can dance. (*He does a little tap dance.*) A voice like syrup of fig. I'm what they used to call a triple threat.

He goes into a boxing crouch, shadow-boxes **Greg**.

Greg   OK, well . . . (*Sitting.*) Sit down a minute, Barry, please, I want to talk to you.

Barry *sits, fidgets.* **Liz** *hands him coffee, he sips.*

Greg   There's just a few things I need to clarify.

Liz   Just a few details.

Barry   (Did I not . . . I gave you all my bank . . . ?)

Liz   Not your bank details . . .

Barry   Is there a problem? (Because you know they always do this. They fuck about with the standing orders . . .)

Greg   No, look –

Barry   (They don't want me to go.)

Greg   Certain things have happened . . .

Barry   What's happened?

Greg   Things in your life. To do with you.

Barry   What about me?

Liz   Interesting things.

Barry   Well, I think we've covered most of it. I think we should just get over there now . . . I'm wasting my juice.

Greg   Well, all the same, I think you should just listen a minute.

Liz   The thing is –

Barry   Sock it to me.

Greg   The thing is, Barry –

Barry   Tell me, what is the thing, John? Because do you know something? Sad to say, I have a better relationship with you people than I do with my own wife these days. Eh? Doing this makes me feel useful. Doing this makes me feel . . . real.

Greg   OK, well, just – there's no easy way to tell you this . . .

Barry   No easy way? I should cocoa. Spit it out.

Greg   Are you listening?

Barry   What? What is it? Yes . . .

Greg   I'm here to question you . . .

Barry   What have I . . . ?

Greg   . . . about a serious criminal offence . . .

Barry   O-ho – yes – *funny* . . .

Greg   Committed in this room and captured on camera
on digital video.

Barry   I . . . what?

Greg   OK. Let's start from day one. Do you know what
I'm talking about?

Barry   . . . ?

Greg   I'm not playing now.

Barry   Y . . . n . . .

Liz   Barry, please, just listen a minute . . .

Greg   This is very serious.

Pause.

Barry   You're . . . are you joking? I don't know what
you're . . . what have I done?

Liz   Greg –

Greg   Just a minute –

Barry   'Greg'? What did you . . . ?

Greg *produces a press ID card.*

Barry   You're . . . wh . . . ?

He studies the card.

Is that real? Who are . . . ?

He stares.

Who are you?

Liz *just stares at her feet.*

Greg   I am in fact the Investigations Editor, OK, you see, and so, you see –

Barry   'The Investigations Editor'?

Greg   For the purposes of this –

Barry   What the fuck?

Greg   – investigation – it was necessary to deploy a certain degree of subterfuge in the name of, of, of –

Barry (*to* **Liz**)   And, and, and, you already knew about this?

Liz *produces her press card.*

Pause.

Barry (*mystified*)   So you're not Ruth's bank manager?

Greg   No.

Long pause.

Barry (*cogs whirring*)   And this has nothing to do with private banking?

Liz   Absolutely nothing.

Barry   Well, now I'm lost.

Greg   Which bit don't you understand?

Barry   I don't understand any of it.

Greg   The thing is, you offered her cocaine.

Barry *looks from one to the other.*

Greg   You offered to purchase cocaine for her.

Barry   Whaaaat?

Greg   I'm afraid you did and my friend here will attest to that.

Liz   (Speed.)

Greg   (Eh?)

Liz   (It was speed.)

Barry   'Speed'? I don't even know what that is. Is that some kind of, of, of drug?

Greg   You did, Barry, and you know how I know you did? Because we've got it on film.

Barry   Film? What film?

Greg   We've got it on videotape.

Barry   I've no idea what you're . . .

Greg *picks up the computer case and shows it to* **Barry**.

Greg   See that?

Barry   What? That little . . . ?

Greg   The little dot?

Barry   What about it?

Greg   Tiny, isn't it?

Barry   Minuscule.

Greg   That's a camera lens. We put a digital camera lens in the case with a radio mike on Liz and there's another one in the bathroom. Amazing, isn't it? Just like James Bond.

Barry *stares.*

Barry   'Liz'?

Greg   All the gadgets.

Barry   I'm confused.

Greg   Well, it's actually pretty straightforward.

Barry   Talk me through it.

Greg   A person, look, a very well-respected member of the public – no, listen – a very close friend of yours, in fact –

Barry   Who?

Greg   Hear me out – in actual fact a very well-respected professional –

Barry   Who?

Greg   – came forward – no, listen – came forward to talk about your situation . . .

Barry   'Situation'?

Greg   About your problem – and so on . . .

Barry   Ruth?

Greg   Because you're not doing your job, Barry . . .

Barry   Ruth? You pay her?

Greg   And you've let down your colleagues and your family and your friends . . .

Barry   That bitch. What would she know about it?

Greg   She worked very closely with us actually . . .

Barry   Let me tell you something about Ruth. Ruth would work with the Nazis if the price was right . . .

Greg   OK, I'd like you to be quite careful what you say to me from here on in . . .

Barry   This is insane! You people are insane! What the bloody fuck . . . ? What the f . . . ?

He stands.

I think if it's all the same to you I really have to be going now . . .

Greg   'Going'? Where are you going?

Barry   I'm going to – all sorts of places.

Greg   But I haven't finished yet.

Barry   Well, I'm a very, a very busy man –

Greg   You picked up the phone and you offered to make a phone call. Am I right? You offered to supply class-A substances to this young woman and that's, you know, that's illegal.

Barry   'Supply'? No –

Greg   Who else have you supplied to, Barry? Other celebrities?

Barry   This is ridiculous.

Greg   It is pretty ridiculous, regrettably, and what's more it's a very serious offence. You're a drunk and a drug addict and a drug supplier and, you know, it's really got to stop.

Barry   You actually said to me – you said to me – she said – she – you – I – I got the distinct impression –

Greg   But you still did it and whether you like it or not my job is to report the facts dispassionately.

Barry   You encouraged me to talk about –

Greg   Do you admit it?

Barry   I think I'll just telephone my agent now please, love, please . . .

Greg   What's your agent going to say?

Liz *passes the telephone to* **Barry**.

Barry   Perhaps I could have a little privacy?

Greg   He's not getting a commission. You were quite specific about that.

Barry   No, no, I didn't say that –

Greg   You just tried to cheat him out of his commission.

Barry   What I actually said was –

Greg   In actual fact, he told me it wasn't really working out with you . . .

Barry   W –

Greg   He's had enough of you, my friend, he was quite clear about that . . .

Barry (*dialling*)   Will you get the fuck out of my face *right now* or I am going to gouge your left eye out with my thumb! (*Brandishing the phone.*) I'll beat you to death with my bare hands and this telephone . . .

Greg   Because you're a bit of a liability is what he said . . .

Barry *hangs up crossly.*

Greg   You asked her to 'touch' you. What was that about?

Barry   I – what?

Greg   Touch you. Earlier. You asked her to touch you. Where did you want her to touch you, Barry?

Barry   I . . . w . . . over there. By the thing.

Greg   That's not what I'm getting at.

Barry   I was off my crust.

Greg   And that makes it acceptable?

Barry   I don't know what you're talking about.

Greg   Do you want to see the film?

Barry   And, and, and even if I did – which I'm not admitting to –

Greg   You did.

Barry   Big deal. What are you, a nun?

Greg   It's not very pleasant, is it?

Barry   It was a *joke.*

Greg   What's funny about it?

Barry   I was just being silly . . .

Greg   And even if it is funny, which I don't think it is, but even if it is (which it really isn't . . .), why does that make it acceptable? Do you follow what I'm trying to say? I mean, for God's sake! What were you thinking?

Barry   I was thinking . . . I *wasn't* thinking.

Greg   Why do you do these things?

Barry   Something just comes over me.

Greg   You were showing off?

Barry   It's my job.

Greg   That's your job, is it? Showing off to girls in hotel rooms and chasing them about like Benny Hill?

Barry   You tricked me. (*To* **Liz**.) I, I, I . . . Remember how I said about my mother – ?

Liz   You said you wanted to be a schoolteacher, yes, I remember.

Greg   They don't want people like you teaching children.

Barry   I could – I'm determined –

Greg   They want good people – they don't want *bad hats* like you.

Barry   I am fucking good!

Greg   No – don't get upset now . . .

Liz   Don't take it personally, Barry . . .

Greg   Don't be such a baby . . .

Liz   There's no need to lose your temper . . .

Barry   Whose side are you on? I confided in you . . .

Liz   Well, I think we all know what that was about . . .

Barry I poured my heart out . . .

Liz Well, I'm sorry about that . . .

Barry We really connected . . .

Liz I honestly didn't mean to 'connect' with you, Barry . . .

Barry I thought you cared, you cow . . .

Liz Well, I don't, I'm sorry, I just don't . . .

Barry All that stuff about the, the, the, the, the, the, the . . . and . . . your, your, your, your, your 'fantasies' . . . ? Eh? And, and, and, and I mean, what was all that about . . . ? I suppose that was supposed to, what, just mindlessly titillate me, I suppose . . . ?

Liz Well, obviously, of course it was, yes.

Greg OK. Let's just park that to one side for a minute. OK. Simmer down now. Because the thing is, see, whether we do this now or not, Barry . . . are you listening? . . . sooner or later somebody is going to run this and, you see, if somebody else gets hold of this . . . one of the other more downmarket publications . . . the shock monkeys . . . you know what they'll write about you, don't you? Family man. Big TV star. Not a very nice person. Mm.

Pause. **Barry** *stares.*

Or . . . you see, with your 'Full Cooperation', I would run a, a, a 'Heartfelt Confession'. You could, you know, just chat to us. Talk about what you're going through. The highs and lows. The mistakes you've made. Eh? All the *emotion.* Talk about your beliefs and feelings. Because a lot of people might be interested to know that behind all the clowning, there's a, you know, there's actually a bit of a, a, a '*dark side*'. Eh? A few, you know, 'demons', as they say. Do you follow what I'm trying to say?

Barry *stares from one to the other.*

Liz   What he's saying is it's for your own good.

Greg   This is exactly the kind of thing people respond to, it's really good stuff.

Barry   Not in my world, chum.

Greg   Well, Barry, you know, I really am sorry but we're not really living in your world any more. We're living in my world. Eh? There's no point in talking to us about your old mum in the Blitz because we can't actually use any of that . . .

Liz   It's just not relevant, Barry . . .

Greg   Now is there anything you don't understand about what we've just said? Because we don't want you to feel you're being pressured here.

Liz   We're trying to be sensitive about this.

Greg   We're absolutely sensitive. Sensitivity is the key.

Pause.

Barry   Well, do I get a fee . . . ?

Greg   'A fee'? Blimey. No, you can't *profit* from it . . . that would be silly.

Barry *goes into the bathroom.*

Greg   Dear oh dear. What is he like? He's bonkers.

He rummages in his camera bag. He produces a tape recorder and microphone.

(*Snorts.*) I loved it when he did that thing with the phone. 'I'll bloody well bash you up with this telephone, mate.' Classic! I nearly pissed myself. Hilarious! I nearly cacked myself. Mind you, he had me going when he tried to get hold of his agent. That's all we need. You were brilliant. You were *brilliant*. That was excellent when you crossed your legs. Phew. It was really convincing. Fuck. This is such a *buzz*. This is so *exciting*. My God . . . I feel *glorious* . . . Sometimes

I feel so, I dunno, constipated . . . but now I just feel so purged and *alive!*

Liz   Do you think he's all right in there? You don't think he's, you know, overdosing or something.

Greg (*snorts*)   I wish!

They listen to various crashes and bangs.

He's looking for the camera. They always do this. Start tearing out the toilet seat and stuff. It's really funny. He'll be out in a minute, looking all wild-eyed . . .

He rummages in his camera bag and produces some crisps, sits, eats.

(*Mouth full.*) I love this job. I love the dressing up. Working up an 'act'. Learning lines. Remembering them. Getting, you know, *butterflies* . . . it's just like being an actor . . .

Liz   Why do you want to be an actor?

Greg   I'm not saying 'I want to be . . .' I'm just . . .

Liz   What's so good about acting?

Greg   It's just really creative and, you know, 'empowering' and you know . . . I just think it's good . . . (Hold still a sec . . .)

Greg *fiddles with the wire under her dress, removes it, adjusts her clothes as they chat.*

Liz   I quite like him, really. He makes me laugh.

Greg   What do you mean?

Liz   He's a funny guy.

Greg   You think he's funny? I don't think he's particularly funny.

Liz   He's quite funny . . .

Greg   You like funny guys. That's just your thing. It doesn't do anything for me. In fact, I'd even go so far as to say I prefer humourlessness. With humourlessness you know where you stand.

Liz *stretches, moves her limbs, bends at the knees, adjusts her clothes.*

Liz   He's really got it, hasn't he?

Greg   What?

Liz   'It.' The 'it' factor.

Greg   I don't see it myself . . .

Liz   Trust me, it's there. I don't know what it is. Charisma. Warmth. 'Inclusiveness.' He just makes you want to be around him. Makes you 'wanna be in his gang'. Don't you think?

Greg   No. You see, that's what happens when you meet famous people. You think you know them. You think you *like* them. You sometimes think they're tremendously *wise*. It's all bullshit. They're fakes. They are, by definition, unknowable and unlikeable – you just can't tell because you don't know them. He's a fucking 'entertainer'. He tells 'good jokes'. He can sing and dance a bit. Big *deal*. They're not important, these people. They're not special. They're *pariahs*. Fame is a cancer. It's a cancer! It's a plague. And it's fucking everywhere. And it's destroying us. And so, you see, it's our responsibility to, you know, just, take him down a peg or two. Eh? Because if we don't . . . yeah? . . . nobody else will.

He starts setting up the tape recorder and directional mike.
Liz *looks in the mirror, turns side-on, examines her figure.*

Liz   Do my tits look too big in this?

Greg   Can tits ever look too big? Eh? (*Snorts.*)

Liz   My breasts mushroom when I'm premenstrual.

Greg   They're fine. They're glorious. (I hadn't even noticed . . .)

Liz   Do you think I look, you know, a bit brassy?

Greg (*staring*)   Eh? 'Brassy'?

Liz   Breasty. Tarty.

Greg   You look marvellous. You're a stunner.

Liz   Do you think I look fat?

Greg   You're a stunner. You're not fat. You're curvy. Curvy is in. Curvy is the new thin. Are you hungry? I'm starving. I could murder a curry. Or a Chinky. You fancy a Chinky? Liz? You fancy a Chinky later? We'll go for a bite, we'll debrief.

Liz   No. I don't want to debrief.

Greg   Oh, you'll debrief all right. You're not going home without debriefing. I'll debrief you if it's the last thing I do. So to speak. Eh?

Liz   What time?

Greg   It doesn't matter what time. Just, you know, do it properly. I'll take you out for dinner. We'll chew the fat.

Liz   Do I have to?

Greg   You don't have to. But you ought to. It'll do you good. And apart from anything else . . . it's the least you can do . . . eh? Sit with me, break bread, break a, a *poppadom*. As they say . . .

Liz   Who says that?

Greg   Eh?

Liz   Who says 'break a poppadom'?

Greg   I don't know . . .

Liz   What does that mean?

Greg   I don't know . . .

Barry *comes out of the bathroom at speed, staring, panting a little.*

Barry   Where's the thing?

Greg Barry –

Barry Where's the, where's the wire . . . ? (*Lunging.*)

Greg Hey – hey – hey –

Liz What did you do that for? That really hurt.

Greg People, please . . .

Liz Did you see that? (Fucking idiot . . .)

Greg (I know it's . . .)

Barry Take your dress off.

Greg Now what's he doing?

Liz Get away from me –

Barry (*grabbing her*) Take your dress off –

Greg What the fuck – ?

Liz You'll rip my – don't you touch me – GET OFF ME – GET HIM OFF OF ME!

Barry *stops. They all stare at each other.*

Blackout.

Act Two

Scene One

Barry *sitting, stares into space.*
Liz *offers* **Barry** *a cigarette from a pack on the table.*
He takes one, lights it, smokes.
Greg *is setting up a mike.*

Greg   All done? Comfy? (*Adjusting mike.*) Excellent. So. (*Very gently now.*) The thing is. (*Pause.*) You are a man who has everything? A wonderful family? Two healthy happy kids in good schools? You're rich? Famous? And yet you show contempt for fame. You show contempt for ordinary people out there who look up to you and will be so disappointed. Because, you see, the thing is, Barry, in the eyes of decent society, your behaviour is not very responsible, is it?

Barry   I haven't done anything.

Greg   Barry, you've done *everything*.

Barry   OK, look . . .

Greg   I'm looking.

Barry   'Greg . . .' It is Greg, isn't it? You know what this is all about? You want 'the scoop'? I'll tell you. *Insurance.* They can't insure me for the next series . . . because I wouldn't take a drugs test.

Greg   Why not, Barry?

Barry   Because it would go on my record I took a drugs test.

Greg   So?

Barry   People would talk. Obviously Ruth must have decided because of –

Greg   Because of a *drugs test?*

Barry   Because nobody would *insure* me. And because I'm not, I'm probably not getting the exact *ratings* or something . . . eh? And that makes me a *terrible person* . . . and so and so now, you see, everybody hates me . . . and now it's all this. (*Pause.*) I made a mistake. *Who cares?*

Liz   'Who cares?' Apart from your wife? After everything she's been through.

Pause.

Barry   My w . . . my wife?

Liz   Do you behave like this at home?

Barry   I . . . sometimes . . .

Greg   What we're saying is that to normal people, to your wife and kids, to people like us . . . people like you are special. You've had a life most people can only dream about and this is how you repay them. By setting a bad example.

Barry   Well, I think you're setting a bad example.

Greg   How's that, Barry?

Barry   People read this spiteful, sneaky bullshit and they think it's OK to be spiteful, sneaky bullshitters.

Greg   Well, I disagree.

Barry   Is that the example you want to set? Is that the kind of world you want to live in?

Greg   OK, well, OK, you see, the point is, you're a pretty morally bankrupt person . . .

Barry   This is ridiculous . . .

Greg   . . . and nobody even realises. And it's time that they did. It's time people knew who you really are, Barry.

Barry   Why?

Greg   Don't you think people have a right to know about you?

Barry Why?

Greg Because if they found out what you were really like they might not find you so funny. And it's in the public interest that they do find out.

Barry What's interesting about it?

Greg It's in the public interest.

Barry Tell me. What's interesting about it? I'm interested . . .

Greg Bec . . . because it's wrong.

Barry Are you – is he serious?

Greg It is! It's against the law.

Barry Are you mad?

Greg And it's, you know, it's bad for you. And it's bad for, you know . . .

Barry Who?

Greg *Society* . . .

Barry How is 'society' going to know?

Greg They'll know when they read it in the paper.

Barry Don't put it in the paper.

Greg I'm sorry?

Barry Don't put it in the paper, you fuckwit.

Greg Are you going to take out an injunction?

Barry You bet your life.

Greg On what grounds?

Barry On the grounds that you're a fuckwit. I'm going to get up a writ and I'm going to have you in chunks . . .

Greg Well, I'm sorry you feel that way about it.

Barry Using the 'privacy laws' . . .

Liz Clause ten in the European Convention on Human Rights, absolutely, the right to privacy.

Greg (Liz . . .)

Liz And clause eight is the right to freedom of expression.

Barry Because . . . what are you expressing?

Liz Sorry?

Barry What are you expressing? You can't even say. What are you expressing? Come on.

Liz *looks blank.*

Barry See? It's like waiting for an egg to boil.

Greg I think that that would be a very dangerous idea, Barry . . .

Barry Really? Enlighten me . . .

Greg Because, you see, I think that would be very harmful . . .

Barry That's the idea . . .

Greg Because, you see, if you take out an injunction –

Barry Harmful to who?

Greg Are you listening . . . ?

Barry Harmful to whom?

Greg If you take out an injunction? You are harming . . . no, listen . . . the *judiciary*. No, don't laugh – because you see if you go around pretending to be 'Mister Saturday Night' when, in reality, you are actually some kind of randy, womanising, drug-addicted bully and you can stop me writing the truth, then anybody can. If you can stop me, Barry, then any old lying, cheating, gerrymandering, arms-dealing, flag-sucking, sadomasochistic, parliamentary wide boy can and that's just not good enough.

Barry   Who did you have in mind?

Greg   The point is you're not who you say you are.

Barry   Who am I?

Greg   You're a hypocrite.

Barry   It takes one to know one. Don't you have anything better to do? If Jesus Christ were alive today you'd be going through his *bins*. What do you get paid to do this? What do they give you, eternal youth?

Liz   You just assaulted me . . .

Barry   Do they teach you to fly?

Liz   You just assaulted me . . .

Barry   I wish I had . . .

Liz   I could've called the police . . .

Greg   What if you do it to somebody else, Barry? Eh? It's not very nice, is it? Because, you see, when people like you do things like that then people like us have no option than to do things like this, otherwise you'll only do it again.

Barry *stares from one to the other.*

Liz   We're not saying you weren't provoked . . .

Greg   There's two sides to everything . . .

Liz   Nobody's saying it's all your fault . . .

Greg   I'm sure everybody understands that you're under a lot of pressure . . .

Liz   Pressure . . .

Greg   And you're in a business where the highs are very high . . .

Liz   Very high, Greg . . .

Greg   But the lows are also pretty, you know, deep . . .

Liz (*simultaneous with 'deep'*)   Low – deep – mm . . .

Greg   I'm sure Valerie does her best. She's only human . . .

Liz   You're only human . . .

Greg   Nobody's perfect . . .

Liz   We're not perfect.

Greg (*gently*)   Would you like to tell us what happened there, Barry? Would you like to talk us through that, because I'm sure people would like to know about that and – I'm sorry, whether you like it or not – it's in your interest that we nail the exact details because otherwise how else do we explain this to your, to your public? Because this is all going to come as quite a, quite a shock to some people. Eh? Can you, can you understand what I'm trying to say?

Barry *stares.*

Barry   W . . . I don't know what you want me to . . .

Greg   No, OK, don't start that again, she told us all about it.

Barry   She . . . who?

Liz   Valerie. Your wife.

Greg   She told us, Barry.

Barry   She . . . ?

Greg   Yes. Yes. Everything. She was very, you know, very forthcoming.

Pause.

Barry (*stares*)   She . . . wouldn't . . . she . . . wouldn't . . .

Greg   She's very worried about you. Says you have a lot of problems, my friend.

Barry   No . . .

Liz   She gave us all the juice, Barry.

Greg   (OK, Liz, just –)

Barry   . . . I don't believe you . . .

Liz   Why don't you ask her?

Barry   I think I'd know if my own wife –

Liz   Then how did we know? How could we know unless she told us?

Barry   Everybody knows . . .

Pause.

Greg   Tell us about Valerie, Barry.

Barry   Look, she's just . . . we're no longer together. OK? We separated. She doesn't like my yolks . . . OK? Is that what you want? You want funnies.

Greg   If you think it's funny.

Barry   I don't really like to talk about it, strangely enough . . .

Liz   Just as a way of simply *understanding* . . . it might help . . .

Greg   Right now, Barry probably needs all the understanding he can get, I'd say, Lizzie . . .

Liz   I'd say so, Greg . . .

Greg   Eh, Barry? Eh, mate?

Pause.

Barry (*stares*)   OK . . . huh . . . (*Pause.*) You see . . . OK . . . she's a bit of a, what we say in the trade, 'difficult to work with'. Erm . . . it's a bit difficult to explain. It's complicated, I put my hand up to that . . .

Liz   What's complicated about it?

Greg   Give it a go.

Long pause.

Barry (*stares, sits*)   She . . . she's found somebody else.
Someone she went to school with. Not from showbiz. A
normal person.

Liz   Well, that's terrible . . .

Barry   Mm. The kids like him. Because he's just an
ordinary bloke, I suppose. They can go to the park, nobody
bothers them.

Greg   So it's pretty serious?

Barry   I, oh, I don't think so . . .

Greg   Still. It just goes to show.

Barry   You see – we've been in 'mediation'. Trying to
thrash out a, a settlement. She wants the house and she'll
get it because of the, because of the kids. But, you see, it's
my house in the first place. I bought it when I was on
LWT . . .

Liz   Are you a good father?

Barry   I – I'm not a bad father . . .

Liz   And yet here you are . . .

Barry   Is this about money? Is that what she . . . ? She
hasn't got any money and so now it's all this . . . ? I'll tell
you something about money. No matter how much you've
got it's never enough. It's never enough.

Greg   When was the last time you took the kiddies to
McDonald's, Barry?

Barry   I'm not allowed to take the kiddies to McDonald's.
They're on diets. When was the last time you took yours?

Greg   That's none of your concern . . .

Barry   See? See how you like it.

Liz   What sort of diets?

Barry   OK. Look . . . she wants custody of the . . . I don't know what to do . . . marvellous, isn't it . . . you have children to take away the, the *bitterness*, that's why we have them, to take away the cynicism – then somebody takes away the children. She's a, she's a lovely woman, you see, but to all intents and purposes, perfectly *nuts*. D'you follow what I . . . ? (*Pause. Staring.*)

Greg   You said earlier that you'd made a mistake. Do you think you've made quite a few mistakes perhaps . . . if you add them up?

Liz   Everybody makes mistakes . . .

Greg   Absolutely . . .

Liz   Would you like to talk about that?

Pause.

Barry   I made some mistakes, absolutely . . .

Greg   Yes – *good* –

Liz   Excellent.

Barry   And I don't know how to put things right . . .

Greg   Mm. Sure. (Into the mike.)

Barry   (Eh?)

Greg   (Into the mike.)

Barry (*into mike*)   I've lost everything. I've lost my wife. My family. My *agent* probably . . .

Greg   You have now.

Barry   I don't really know what to do.

Liz   I really liked what you said about how you loved the ordinary people, the ordinary fans, the nurses and the teachers. Do you think they might still love you? Even after everything you've done?

Barry   I . . .

Greg Even after all of this?

Barry I . . . I hope so.

Liz Do you still love them?

Barry Y . . . I think . . .

Liz Then why did you do what you did?

Barry I . . . I don't know.

Greg Would you say you were an angry person?

Barry I can get angry . . .

Liz We've seen that. And some of the things you said about your fans . . . you said they were 'deformed', and 'speccy', you said that some of them had been 'lobotomised' . . . that's quite *cruel*, isn't it?

Barry Mm . . .

Liz Quite callous.

Barry Mm . . .

Liz Do you think the pain in people's lives is funny?

Barry *just stares.*

Liz Do you think the darkness in people's lives is funny?

Barry *just stares.*

Greg Don't you think it's time you grew up? (*Pause*) Do you have any regrets?

Barry Yeah . . . I have a few.

Greg What do you regret?

Barry Everything.

Greg Do you regret what happened with Valerie?

Barry I regret what happened there, obviously, and with my . . . with my kids. I miss them all the time. I just . . . miss them . . .

Greg   Well, we can see that . . .

Pause.

Barry   Sometimes I wonder whether I . . . whether I drove her away. Something did. The pressures of fame perhaps. The pressures of fame on me, obviously, which, indirectly, I expect she bore the brunt of . . .

Liz   And how does that make you feel? About your fame? Do you –

Barry   Well. I'm very annoyed. Obviously.

Liz   Do you blame fame?

Barry   W . . . how do you mean?

Liz   For what's happened to you. Do you blame fame?

Barry   N . . . yeah, yes. I do. As a matter of fact.

Liz   You blame fame.

Barry   I blame fame.

Liz   The 'fame game'.

Barry   Yes.

Liz   You blame . . . ?

Barry   I blame the f . . . the fame game. Mm. It's like a, a, a drug, you see. It's more like a drug than . . . than drugs!

Greg   Excellent. Oh, that's very good.

Liz   So you don't blame yourself.

Barry   I blame myself a bit too. It's a sort of two-pronged attack . . .

Greg   And what would you like to say to all those people who looked up to you and respected you, who you've betrayed now?

Barry   I'd just . . . I'd just . . . I'd like to say I'm, you know, I'm sorry and all that.

Liz   You don't seem very sorry. Don't you feel ashamed?

Barry   Uh?

Greg   'Ashamed.' Aren't you terribly ashamed by what's been going on?

Barry   I am. Yes. I am ashamed.

Liz   How ashamed?

Barry   Very ashamed.

Greg   How do you hope that people will respond to this dreadful news? When they buy the paper with their hard-earned money and they open the paper and it's all, you know, they have to read all this? How do you think they'll feel? How would you like them to respond? With compassion?

Barry   I'd . . . I'd hope . . .

Greg   Well, do you think you can change?

Barry   I don't know.

Liz   Would you like to try?

Barry   Y . . . yes. (*Into mike.*) I'll certainly give it a go . . .

Greg   And what happens if you aren't able to change? What happens if, say, if Valerie or your kids ask you to change but you still can't stop . . . what would happen then?

Pause.

Barry   I'd rather, I'd rather . . . you know, I should think my life wouldn't be worth living.

Greg   I see, so you'd rather . . . what does that mean? 'Life wouldn't be worth living.' What does . . . ?

Barry   It means what . . . what I just said. It means what it means.

Greg   I see – so – I'm sorry – I have to ask these questions
– are you saying – what are you actually saying? That if that
happened, you'd rather . . . ?

Barry   In a, in a funny way, maybe, I would rather . . .
not go on living . . . mm . . .

Greg   You'd rather 'not go on living' . . . What does that
. . . does that mean you'd rather, what, you'd rather – ?

Barry   I'd rather –

Greg   You'd rather 'die' . . . ? (*Pause.*) And that's a solemn
vow.

Barry   That's a solemn vow.

Greg   On your children's lives?

Barry   On my children . . . on my . . . on my k . . . on my
kids' . . .

He stares into space. He puts his head in his hands, sniffs, wipes eyes.

Greg   Excellent. This is really good stuff, Barry. Are you
ready to do some pictures now?

Greg *takes a camera from the bag and changes lenses.*

Barry   No, come on now. Look at me. I'm welling up
now . . .

He turns away. Wipes his eyes, sniffs. Blows his nose.

Greg   It's all right, take your time . . .

Barry *raises a glass to drink.* **Greg** *raises the camera to take a shot.*
Barry *lowers the glass without drinking.*

Greg   That's right, with the, with the glass . . .

Barry *raises the glass to drink again.* **Greg** *raises the camera to take
a shot.* **Barry** *lowers the glass.*

Beat.

Barry *raises the glass and quickly lowers it.* **Greg** *simultaneously does the same with the camera.*

Greg   How about a cigarette?

Liz *offers him a ciggie.*
Greg *takes flash photos.* **Barry** *doesn't respond.*

Greg   Just, turn your head to – no, towards me . . . splendid . . .

Flash photos.

Barry   OK, well, anyway I think I'd like to just call my legal representative now please . . .

Greg   . . . Sorry?

Barry   Well, erm, he probably ought to know about this . . . I'm not so sure about making vows . . .

Greg   We won't hold you to it . . .

Barry *puts the glass down.*

Barry   I'm not supposed to be drinking . . .

Liz   Well, Barry, you had things from the minibar . . .

Greg   And yes, and, you see, no, because I couldn't stop you . . . could you, Liz – ?

Barry *(picking up phone)*   Well, anyway, I'm calling Kevin just to be on the safe side.

Greg   You helped yourself to drinks from the minibar and then you threatened me and then you assaulted her.

Liz   D'you want me to 'legal it', Barry?

Greg   (OK, Liz . . .)

Liz   I'll get on the phone now, legal the story, it's 'zoo time'.

Greg   (Don't say 'legal it', OK? And, and don't say 'zoo time'. It's, it's meaningless . . .)

Liz (OK. Sorry . . .)

Barry (*dialling*)   Are you done? (*Into phone.*) Hello, Kevin? I'm sorry. Oh, do please excuse me. (*Hangs up.*) How do I get an outside line on this?

Greg We'll get to that . . .

Barry (*dialling, to* **Liz**)   Is it 9 or 0?

Liz Why was Valerie in hospital, Barry?

Barry (*into phone*)   Kev . . . ? I'm so sorry, my love. Can I possibly speak to Kevin ever so briefly? This is rather urgent . . . no, OK, no, I'll . . . I'll hold. Marvellous. Thank you, dear . . . (*He waits.*)

Greg Why was your wife in hospital, Barry?

Barry Hospital? What hospital?

Greg That hospital that your wife was in. Is that why she left you?

Barry No – no – no –

Greg No – hold on –

Barry She's been very ill.

Greg I know she has, I know, Barry, and why is she ill?

Barry I . . . I don't know . . . nobody really knows. It's just one of those things.

Greg Just one of those things. OK, well, you see the thing is, she's been under a lot of pressure, hasn't she, Barry? A lot of stress, a lot of strain . . .

Barry Y . . . well . . . we both have, yeah . . .

Greg And you say your behaviour might have contributed?

Barry . . . Sorry?

Greg   The stress you have caused might have contributed to her illness?

Barry   It's a sort of vicious circle . . .

Liz   It is rather vicious, isn't it, Barry? Eh? Don't talk about your fame, don't talk about your lawyer, eh? You, you big *bully*. Eh? What did you do to her?

Barry   W . . . I don't know what you're talking about.

Greg   Well, I think you do.

Barry   She found a lump.

Pause.

Greg   A, a, a . . . how do you mean?

Barry   She found a lump . . . she had a biopsy . . . we thought it was a cyst . . . she started getting these pains . . . she went into hospital for tests, at Christmas, just for a, just for a scan. Then it was the, you know, the barium enema and the . . . we went private, went first class, do it properly. Well, there's no messing around then. It's all been a bit sudden . . .

Liz   Why didn't you tell us all this?

Barry   Well, I don't tell you *everything*. It's none of your business. (*Phone.*) Kevin, my dear, dear friend. How the fucking hell are you . . . ?

He takes the phone to the bathroom. The cord doesn't quite reach. He puts the phone on the floor and takes the handset into the bathroom and shuts the door.

Pause.

Greg   Fuuuuuck.

Pause.

Liz   Good story though . . .

Greg It's a great story. In fact, it's a, it's probably a *better* story . . . The *divorce* . . . the kiddies . . . (I know what that's like.)

Liz (OK, Greg . . .)

Greg (When there's children involved, Lizzie –)

Liz (Whatever . . .)

Greg And now she's having all these problems, health prob – no, don't laugh, this is what happens as you get older . . .

Liz Oh please.

Greg It's really sad . . .

Liz Yes. 'Sad.' Excellent . . .

Greg . . . It really is, it's a, it's tragic . . . I mean . . .

Liz 'Tragic', good. I like that . . . (*Removing her wig.*) (God, look at my hair.)

Greg A perfectly ordinary, *normal* woman . . . married to a brilliant, gifted entertainer, an irresistible double act – inseparable for all those years right up until the tragic end – which is when the strain began to show a bit and she ran off with somebody else. It's perfectly understandable.

Liz *concentrates on removing her make-up in the mirror.*

Liz Simple and effective.

Greg Simple and at the same . . . uniquely complex.

Liz Two uniquely complex people . . .

Greg In *his* pain he turned to . . .

Liz Unable to *face* it he regrettably found himself turning to . . .

Greg Yes, yes, but only because of *her* pain . . .

Liz Absolutely. Or: he didn't even care.

Greg   How do you mean?

Liz   Maybe he didn't even feel any pain. That's the kind of person he is. They had everything *and yet* . . . even as she lay dying, he was in a five-star luxury hotel room snorting large amounts of fucking hard drugs . . . eh? Propositioning young *women*. Eh?

Greg   O-ho. Cynical.

Liz   People like cynicism.

Greg   It's risky.

Liz   I like the risk.

Greg   What if he's lying? He's so manipulative . . .

Liz   We could check with the hospital . . .

Greg   Check it with Valerie . . .

Liz   I'm not checking with her . . .

Greg   Check it with her and we'll know what we've got.

He goes to the bathroom door, listens.

Shit. What are they talking about?

He examines the phone on the floor.

Should I just . . . I could cut him off or something?

He dithers.

What if he's talking to Valerie? I could just . . .

He picks up phone cradle, considers.

Liz   Well, go on.

Greg   You think I should?

He gingerly pulls the phone cradle away from the door and puts it down again, dithering.

Liz   Go on.

The phone moves back towards the door as **Barry** *tugs on the cord from the other side.*

Just do it.

Greg *reaches out, is about to cut it off when the phone is dragged another foot away from him and he gives up.*

Greg   I can't do it . . .

He comes back and sits.

I feel a bit sorry for him really . . .

Liz   What do you mean?

Greg   I'm saying . . . I just . . . I feel sorry for him now.

Liz   I don't understand what you mean.

Greg   Well, don't you?

Liz (*blank, mystified*)   Don't I what?

Greg   Feel a bit sorry for him?

Liz   No. He's an idiot.

Greg   Exactly. He's just an idiot. It's not against the law to be an idiot.

Liz   And it's not against the law to call him an idiot. He knows what he's doing.

Greg   His wife is dying.

Liz   Well, he should have thought of that before.

Greg   Before what?

Liz   Before he became famous and started acting like this. It's no use crying to us. Just because some relative – OK, his wife or whatever – may or may not be rather ill – which we don't know for a fact – it could well change – she might make a full recovery – she might be in remission as we speak – but does this make his behaviour excusable?

She produces a mobile phone and dials.

Hiya, Valerie, it's Liz. 'Lizabeth from the newspaper. How
are you? I'm very-very-well indeed thank you very much.
Busy-busy-busy. Still at it. Mm. Ha ha. How are the ponies?
(*Pause.*) Oh, they're quarter-horses, really? Quarter-horses,
twice the fun. Ha ha. (*Pause, moving on.*) OK, well, anyway,
what I wanted to talk to you about . . . mm . . . I saw him
this evening . . . mm . . . well, to be perfectly honest he was
a bit on the . . . you could sort of smell it . . . on his breath,
mm . . . well, you see, Valerie, I am rather concerned . . .
yes, I know you are, I am too . . . just a little anxious . . .
well, you see, he's been saying some rather disturbing things
. . . about you actually . . . well, he said you'd been very
poorly . . . mm . . . mm . . . which is something I didn't . . .
no I didn't . . . I didn't know that either . . . really? You
poor thing . . . actually, have you got a minute? (*Pause.*) No,
OK, sure, that's absolutely . . . OK . . . bye-bye . . . take
care . . . bye-bye . . .

She hangs up, stares.

Greg   Is she OK?

Liz   Irritable bowel syndrome.

Greg   Irr . . . wh . . . ?

Liz   That's what she said.

Greg   W . . . was she joking?

Liz   I don't think so. That's what she's got. IBS.

Greg   Oh . . .

Liz   Yes. 'Oh . . .'

Greg   That's a pity.

Pause.

Liz   Well, it's probably still pretty unpleasant, Greg.

Greg   Mm. Oh. Very uncomfortable.

Liz   And quite worrying, I should imagine.

Greg   Some people die if they eat nuts . . .

Liz   I know, and he doesn't even care. He doesn't.

Pause.

Greg   D'you think she's lying?

Liz   I . . . no. I think it's more likely he's lying.

Greg   D'you think it's a wind-up?

Liz   Maybe they're both liars.

Greg   Well, that's just wrong.

Liz   Yes and I'm sorry but no, that's just not on.

Greg   I'm sorry.

Liz   That's just rude.

Greg   It's not very helpful.

Liz   Now what are we supposed to do?

Barry *comes back in, replaces the phone, examines himself in the mirror, straightens his tie, smoothes his clothes.*

Barry   OK. So. Here's the situation –

Liz   Why was your wife really in hospital, Barry?

Barry   This is my position –

Liz   Really, for real. In real life. What did you do to her?

Barry   My position is this –

Liz   Did you lose your temper . . . ?

Barry   What I think –

Liz   Did you lose your temper with her . . . ?

Barry   What I think is that this is 'slander' . . .

Liz   Well, I disagree, because, you see, I think that there's something you're not telling us here . . .

Barry   And if you write it then it's 'libel' . . .

Liz   Because we've talked to Valerie.

Barry   And what you just did, love, is called 'entrapment'. OK? And Kevin my lawyer just spent all week in the High Court and he loves it there, he's really good at it, and so, you see, now I'm going to get a writ and sue you . . .

Liz   I phoned Valerie and –

Barry   And the next time I see you will be in the High Court –

Greg   Barry – just –

Liz   I phoned Valerie –

Barry   Because I'll tell you another thing –

Greg   OK, let's just –

Barry   You picked the wrong guy to do this to –

Greg   Settle down now –

Barry   OK, but you picked the wrong guy.

Greg   OK.

Barry   You think I'm bullshitting? You think everybody's bullshitting. Because you're a bullshitter and so you assume that everybody else is too . . .

Liz   I phoned Valerie. She didn't say anything about a biopsy.

Barry   Well, are you surprised?

Liz   Why didn't she, OK, then, why didn't she tell us . . . ?

Barry   BECAUSE IT'S PRIVATE! DON'T YOU UNDERSTAND? IT'S PRIVATE! IT'S PRIVATE! YOU STUPID BITCH – JESUS! (*Pause.*) Tell me something. Does it bother you being so dumb? Because that's, you see, I think that's the problem here. The trouble is that you have no imagination . . . you have zero imagination . . . and so humanity is a mystery to you . . . the stink of your own spleen and bile – the pain you inflict – is a mystery to you . . . you people . . . I don't think you know what you do. I don't think you know what you do. And that's a very frightening thing. (*Pause.*) Is my life worth so little? Is my life worth so little now that unless I'm in the paper, making a fool of myself, I'm, what, no good to anyone any more?

Greg   Anyway, getting back to what we were talking about . . .

Barry   You think I'm a schmuck?

Liz   Please –

Barry   Sue you? I should kill you! Then you'd learn.

Greg   I've no doubt you're quite capable of that, Baz –

Barry (*going over to* **Greg**)   You think this is funny? I'll show you something funny . . . I'll show you something funny . . . I'll show you something funny, eh?

Barry *grabs him by the elbow, drags him to one side.*

Greg   Wait – wait – wait – wait – wait – wait – wait – wait –

Barry (*squeezing* **Greg***'s balls*)   If you ever come near me or my family again I'm going to get hold of you and I'm going to shoot you in the balls.

Barry *spits on the floor and goes.*
They stare.
Silence.

Greg   OK. Look. OK. Look. OK. Look. OK. Look. OK. Look. There is actually an editorial issue here. The issue being that – we have no idea what's going on – and – if we don't get our story straight – we're going to look foolish. We'll have to spike the story or he'll get up a writ and sue the paper – cost him two hundred pounds – no, listen to me – I believe him.

Liz We've still got the tape . . .

Greg How much did he drink? How pissed was he . . . ?

Liz You know how pissed he was . . .

Greg Then it's tainted evidence – it really is entrapment – and now I'm going to lose my job – because you fucked it up – and it was my idea – and, and, and I'm the eldest . . .

Liz You won't lose your job.

Greg Liz, the PCC –

Liz Oh, fuck the PCC –

Greg I'm on the PCC! I've got a family to feed. This is how I put food on the table.

Liz Face it Greg – they all hate you.

Greg That's none of your business.

Liz You're not even trying now. Why don't you just go after him and lick his arsehole?

Pause.

Greg (Why don't I just lick yours?)

Liz (Sorry . . . ?)

Greg (Why don't I lick yours?)

Pause.

Liz (Don't be revolting.) Just pull yourself together . . . (*Pause.*) Are you listening to me? Greg? (*Producing mobile phone.*) I'm going to legal it –

Greg WILL YOU STOP SAYING THAT! (*Grabbing her phone.*)

Liz If you can't stand the heat then go back to the *Wandsworth Guardian* and raise money for charity – buy your local hospital a new incubator – go to church fêtes and stare at prize marrows until your fucking eyeballs bleed . . .

Greg   OK, shut up . . .

Liz   What on earth has happened to you?

Greg   Shut up, Liz . . .

Liz   What did he do to you? Just calm down –

Greg   I AM PERFECTLY FUCKING CALM!

Blackout.

Scene Two

Barry *in a tracksuit.*
Liz *dressed casually.*

Liz   It's just such a shock.

Barry   It was . . . very . . . sudden.

Liz   God. I know.

Barry   Yes.

Liz   God.

Pause.

Barry   She went back into hospital just after you . . . it was everywhere, you know . . . nothing they could do . . . (*Gestures.*) She went home for a while and they put her on a, you know they gave her oxygen in a tank which helped for a bit but she had so little . . . (*Gestures. Stares.*) She didn't want to go into a hospice, you see . . . she wanted to be at home with . . . with her . . . ponies. I'd go round there a bit just to keep her company . . . comfort her when she . . . she sometimes would . . . cry in the night and so on . . . she couldn't sleep . . . she'd just be thinking about . . . I'd hear her crying to herself quietly and . . . uh, broke my heart really . . . She was just . . . very frightened, you see . . . poor old thing . . . (*Pause.*) I'd try and be there to hold her hand. Give her a cuddle and cheer her up a bit . . . I took her out a bit when she wanted to get some air. I took her around a few of the old . . . all her favourite places . . . took her for a curry, to her favourite curry place down in the village, she wanted to say hi, or bye . . . but you know there was no tables, you see, we couldn't get a table and nobody was, nobody she knew was on that night and so it was a bit of a . . . it was just a . . . uh . . . I felt so sorry for. She was just being friendly. She just wanted to say goodbye. (*Pause.*) I took her to the market . . . took her around all the old stalls, the cheese stall, the flower stall, the fishmonger, you know the kind of . . . so she could tell them. Tell them she was actually going to die and all that. They didn't believe her. I told them, I said . . . (*Gestures.*) They didn't believe me. Thought I was joking. Typical. (*Pause.*) So you see it was all very . . . six weeks it took. Seventeen years of marriage all gone in . . . (*Pause.*) It was . . . very, very sad really . . . very sad.

Liz   Would you like a banana? They're good for you.

She hands him a banana from the fruit bowl.
She takes one too.

Barry   Mm. Packed with zinc.

Liz   I know it's . . .

Barry   Good for the nut.

Liz   Mm.

Barry   Full of antioxidants. I'm an expert on all that now . . .

He peels his banana.
Liz *peels hers.*
Silence.

Liz   It must have been unimaginably awful . . .

Barry   Yeah, yes, it was. Unimaginably . . .

Liz   I can't imagine what you went through . . .

Barry   No, I know you can't . . . (*He takes a bite.*)

Pause. She takes a bite.

Liz   At least you'd had a chance to, you know, say your peace and all that. At least you'd had a chance to, you know, make amends.

Barry   In our fashion, I suppose . . .

Liz   . . . I think you probably did.

Barry   Mm. Well . . .

They eat. He is becoming emotional, gesturing with the banana between bites.

Technically speaking she'd filed for divorce. I'd thought maybe I could talk her out of it. But I couldn't change her mind after . . . (*Pause.*) She was all the more determined . . . once they make their minds up, you see, the good ones, there's no going back.

They eat in silence.

Liz   Thanks for meeting me. (*Pause.*) It's very kind of you. (*Pause.*) After all the . . . you know . . . (*Pause.*) Greg lost his job. (*Pause.*) I got a pay rise . . . (*Pause.*) I bought a car. A Mini. (*Mimes 'driving'.*) Are you all right?

Barry   You . . . you don't know what you did. Her last few weeks . . . you took away her . . . will to . . . her dignity, you see. The strain, you see. The stress. Calling her up all hours . . . accusing me . . . accusing me of . . . you don't know what it did to her . . .

Liz   Well, Barry, you know . . . she was quite, she was probably quite ill before I came along . . .

Barry   She wasn't fucking dying before you came along!

Liz   I didn't come here to argue . . .

Barry Well, I did. I came here to argue. Come on, let's argue. (*Pause.*) They axed my show.

Liz I'm sorry about the show . . . it was so –

Barry No you're not.

Pause.

Liz I never wanted to do this, you know. I wanted to be a music critic . . . or a, you know, a rock journalist . . .

Barry Yeah, really 'make a difference' . . . Really 'give something back . . .'

Liz You don't know what I'm really like.

Barry O-ho, I think I do . . .

Liz You don't know what I think about or what I, you know, really care about . . . don't laugh . . . don't laugh at me . . . I know you think I'm 'shallow'. You're entitled to your –

Barry Entitled to my opinion? What's it got to do with opinion?

Pause.

Liz I'm not shallow . . .

Barry You're so shallow you're evaporating . . .

Liz Well, I'm trying to say I'm sorry . . .

Barry Mm-hmm – is it going to take long . . . ? (*Checks his watch.*)

Liz I just want you to be happy now . . .

Barry Do I *look* happy? (*Snorts.*) Jesus. How *likely* do you think that is?

Pause.

Liz I'm just . . . so sorry now . . . I don't know what to . . .

Silence.
Barry *takes milk from the minibar and drains most of it.*

Pause.

Barry   My dearest wish . . . I wish I could say: 'My wife . . .
my loving wife . . . she loved me . . . we had a good
innings.' I'd give anything. The nicest, gentlest, dearest
woman. The dearest woman. It was a priv . . . a privilege to
have known her.

He finishes his banana and drops the skin on the floor.
She puts hers down without finishing.

Liz   I know how much you two people really meant to
each other. I know you loved her very dearly.

Barry   Yes, yeah, I did.

He sits and drinks milk.

Liz   And she loved you very dearly.

Barry   Y . . . well . . . (you know . . .)

Liz   She did. And if you don't mind me saying (knowing
her as I did –)

Barry   (Well, you –)

Liz   You came back from all sorts of terrible . . . personal
. . . I mean, you were bonkers. You! Cor! You were mad for
it!

Pause.

Barry   I don't do that any more. I don't drink.

Liz   None of my business.

Barry   I don't.

Liz   Even if you did –

Barry   I don't.

Liz   Even if you did –

Barry   Well, I don't. I stopped.

Liz   OK. Good. As a mark of respect.

Barry   I stopped because I wouldn't have been able to handle it.

Liz   *And* as a mark of respect.

Barry   Because I would have probably gone insane. Waiting about in that hospital day and night. Waiting for the end. I had to be . . . I had to be fit. For Valerie. For the kids . . .

Liz   Exactly. Respect for your, for your family –

Barry   I even went to the gym. That's how much I . . . that's how scared I was . . . I don't get depressed any more.

Liz   You feel you've atoned?

Barry   Eh?

Liz   You feel you've *atoned?*

Barry   I'm quite toned, yeah, I haven't let myself go. I swim a lot . . .

Liz   You don't get depressed any more. Why?

Barry   Well, you see, to put it bluntly . . . because I'm alive, love. What have I got to be depressed about? To put it brutally, I'm not lying flat on my back being slowly suffocated to death. It's like I've got a, a . . .

Liz   A second chance.

Barry   Well . . .

Liz   A new lease on life.

Barry   I pulled myself together a bit, yeah.

Liz   Do you think she knows?

Pause.

Barry   How would she know?

Liz   Do you think she's, you know, watching you?

Barry   How d'you mean?

Liz   From above. Do you think she's perhaps watching over you?

Pause.

Barry (*staring*)   I doubt it, love.

Liz   How do you know? She might be. How else do you explain it? You're a reformed character. It's a miracle.

Barry   I just –

Liz   If there's any consolation this is it.

Barry   What?

Liz   In a sense you could say that by, that – almost – by dying, Valerie basically, in a sense, saved you.

Pause.

Barry   Oh, OK, well, I see where you're coming from . . .

They stare at each other.

Silence.

Liz   Could I qu . . . could I, you know, quote you on this?

Barry   W. . . ?

Liz   Could I, could I, sort of, I'm saying . . . just in case I do a piece . . . just a small piece . . .

Pause.

Barry   I'd rather you didn't.

Liz   Fine, fine, no obviously –

Barry   I thought you –

Liz   No, I know you came to –

Barry   You said you wanted to –

Liz Pay my, yes, pay my respects. Give my, you know, condolences. And all that. Mm. (You've got a little bit of . . .) (*She gestures.*)

He wipes away a milk moustache.

(Hang on . . .)

Barry (I get it?)

Liz (*wipes*) (I got it.)

Silence.

I was only going to say – you know – if you don't mind me saying – I'm sorry but I really have to say this – I think it's a very special story and what's more a, a very moving story and I would like very much if you could find it in yourself to allow me to share, to *share* this very *private* story . . .

Barry Share it with who?

Liz With everybody.

Pause.

Barry No, if it's all the same, I think I'll be on my way . . .

Liz Are you going home?

Barry Yes, I've got the car and I'll just . . . you know . . . have a biscuit and go to bed.

Liz Well, I really think we should do this. For, you know, if not for you then for V . . . Valerie . . . and at least . . . for the *children* . . .

Pause.

Barry No, I'd just as soon keep my powder dry.

Liz (*gently*) OK. Good. That's all right. That's fine. (*Pause.*) I'm only saying, you know, I don't know what *your* memories are but *my* memories, most people's memories of you two are pretty, you know . . . (*Pause.*) I think people think you,

you know, had your differences . . . I think they think you
had your ups and downs . . . I think they think you perhaps
didn't like each other a whole lot sometimes . . . perhaps you
weren't very nice to each other sometimes . . . and so they
draw the wrong conclusions . . .

Pause.

Barry   Well, all the same, I'd rather just be left alone now.

Liz   But, you see, only the other day I was saying to my
features editor – who absolutely agrees with me on this by
the way – which is nice –

Barry (*stands*)   Could I just . . . get back to you on this?

Liz   Well, if you need reassuring . . .

She produces a mobile phone.

Barry   I don't . . .

Liz   I know how much she loved you. I know she *adored*
you . . . deep down. I know she *forgave* you. She didn't want
to leave you.

Pause.

Barry   She . . . ? How do you know?

Liz (*dials*)   It's *obvious*. She loved you to bits. (Hold on.
Answerphone. I'll text.)

She texts.
He hovers.

Barry (*staring*)   I remember once she told me, she said,
she'd never wanted anybody else.

Liz (*simultaneous with 'else'*)   Never even wanted anybody
else, well, there you go . . .

Barry   One of the last things she said: she never even
looked at anybody else. Not seriously . . .

Liz   And why would she?

Barry   It, it haunts me to this day . . . I had this dream about her . . . I dream about her every night . . .

Liz (*texting, not listening*)   Mm, I know . . . that's right . . .

Barry   It's always the same dream . . . every single night . . . I dream she's still here . . . or she's come back somehow . . . but, you see, she's terrifically old, for some reason, a little old lady. A happy little old lady. Like my mum. Older than me. I'm like her toyboy. And I take her in my arms . . . it's so good to hold her, just to hold her, she's very warm . . . it doesn't matter that she's so old, it's still her as far as I'm concerned . . . the only trouble is, she's so old and frail, I'm afraid she's going to kick the bucket again.

Liz   Well, it's time to put the record straight. This is a, you know, a really great love story.

Barry   You know . . . my kids . . . my children . . . are the only people who've ever . . . (*Pause.*) People talk about being a single mother . . . being a single father isn't a million laughs . . .

Liz   Well, anyway, I really believe in this. I'm passionate about it. I can, you know, really make it happen . . .

Barry   You . . . ?

Liz   And I can get you a really good *fee*.

Her phone rings.
Barry *stares into space.*

Liz   Get you a decent chunk of . . . probably spread it over two consecutive . . . you know . . . (*Into phone.*) Hi, hi-ya. I'm here now. Oh. Is she at lunch? Again? Greedy bitch. Ha ha. No. No, don't tell her . . . ha ha ha, you know what she's like . . . 'sensitive', I know . . . ha ha ha ha . . . I know, she gets so cross . . . no, yeah, I'll . . . oh, has she? Great. Put her on. (*Gives thumbs up to* **Barry**.) Hi, it's me. Liz. Yeah I'm here now. He's with me now. Absolutely fine. Absolutely. Hold on. (*She offers the phone to* **Barry**.) Go for it. Go on. (*Into phone.*) I'm going to put him on.

She offers phone to **Barry**.
He hesitates.

For the children. Barry. For the children.

She offers the phone again.
He takes the phone, stares at it, puts it to his ear, still hesitates,
confused.
She gives him the thumbs up.

Barry   What sort of fee are we talking about?

Blackout.

Lightning Source UK Ltd.
Milton Keynes UK
UKOW040744290513

211408UK00001B/7/P